P9-DND-801

P. Allen Smith's

COLORS
FOR THE GARDEN

P. Allen Smith's

COLORS
FOR THE GARDEN

Creating Compelling Color Themes

PHOTOGRAPHS BY JANE COLCLASURE

ILLUSTRATIONS BY P. ALLEN SMITH

DESIGN BY DINA DELL'ARCIPRETE/dk DESIGN PARTNERS INC

CLARKSON POTTER/PUBLISHERS
New York

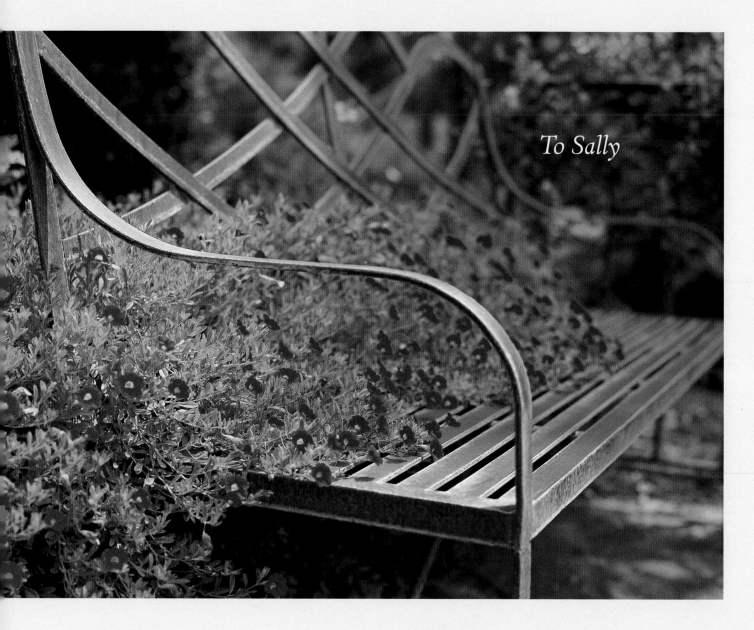

To Sally

Copyright © 2006 by Hortus, Ltd.

All rights reserved.
Published in the United States by Clarkson Potter/Publishers, an imprint of the Crown Publishing Group, a division of Random House, Inc., New York.
www.crownpublishing.com
www.clarksonpotter.com

Clarkson N. Potter is a trademark and Potter and colophon are registered trademarks of Random House, Inc.

Library of Congress Cataloging-in-Publication Data
Smith, P. Allen.
P. Allen Smith's colors for the garden: creating compelling color themes /
P. Allen Smith.—1st ed.   1. Color in gardening.   I. Title: Colors for the garden.   II. Title.
SB454.3.C64S65   2006
635.9′68—dc22

ISBN13: 978-1-4000-5342-1
ISBN10: 1-4000-5342-0

Printed in Japan

10   9   8   7   6   5   4   3   2   1

First Edition

ACKNOWLEDGMENTS

Like the kaleidoscope of color we find in the garden, a myriad of talents and the dedication of many people contributed to the creation of this book.

First and foremost, I am very grateful to Betsy Lyman, whose excitement for this topic has been unwavering. Her thoughtful insight, organizational skills, and creative energy kept the project on course. Without her tireless assistance and encouragement, this book would have never hit the shelves.

I owe many thanks to Betty Freeze, who not only assisted me in the garden, but also helped assemble the plant lists and directory. I thank Frances Cheshire, whose assistance in organizing and scanning photographs helped enormously; Nicole Claas, whose creative talents aided me in styling our photo sessions; and Mary Ellen Pyle, who proofed many versions of the text. And, of course, this book could not exist without Jane Colclasure's stunning photographs. Her eye captured so beautifully the colors of the garden and the individual flowers themselves.

I am especially fortunate to have had the enthusiastic support from the beginning of this project from my publisher, Lauren Shakely, and editorial director, Pam Krauss. I am extremely indebted to the entire staff at Clarkson Potter for their encouragement to create such a visually rich book: to my editors, Natalie Kaire, Jennifer Defilippi, and Elissa Altman for their direction through the manuscript; to Marysarah Quinn, Jane Treuhaft, and Dina Dell'Arciprete, for their enlightened sense of design and style; to Mark McCauslin, Merri Ann Morrell, and Joan Denman, for shepherding the book through production; to Tina Constable, Tammy Blake, and Campbell Wharton, for their enthusiasm and tireless efforts at getting the word out about the book.

I also want to thank all of my friends and clients who have allowed me the pleasure of creating colorful gardens with them over the years, and especially those who have opened their homes and gardens for the creation of this book: Rick Smith and Susan Sims Smith, Judge Robert and Mary Lynn Dudley, Mark and Kim Brockinton, Dr. Reed and Rebecca Thompson, Jim Dyke and Helen Porter, Sally Foley, Jay and Patsy Hill, Warren and Harriet Stephens, Nancy and Cason Callaway, Mike Mayton and Cathy Hamilton Mayton, Robert and Gaye Anderson, Overton and Kaye Anderson, Claiborne and Elaine Deming, Henry and Marilyn Lile, Viscount and Viscountess Ashbrook, Charles and Jane Foster, Beds and Borders, and Dr. Milton and Janee Waner.

Of the many individuals who have contributed their talents and time, I would like to thank in particular: Ken and Ellen Hughes, Richard and Susan Wright and Sawyer and Graceleigh Wright, Margaret Litton, Phoebe Wesinger, Maynard Hannah, Susan Henry, Carl Miller, Kathy Graves, Doug Buford, Elba Benitez, Ronnie Chapman, and Norma Ryals.

I am also thankful to my entire staff at Hortus, Ltd., who each day played an important role in the development of this book and who continue to communicate the ideas and principles behind it: Ward Lile, Pam Holden, Jefferson Davis, Mandy Shoptaw, Todd Orr, David Curran, Bill Reishtein, Shelby Brewer, Sarah Burr, and Keith Freeman.

Also, I thank a long list of institutions and companies that have backed this book in so many ways: Sherwin Williams, Napp Deady, Aschla, New England Pottery, Summer Classics, Magnolia Casual, Lazy Hill, Norcal, Lane Venture, Gilbert Wild and Sons, Renee's Garden, the Full Moon, Cobblestone and Vine, Cantrell Gardens, Hocott's Garden Center, Lakewood Garden Center, Chicago Botanic, Old Westbury Gardens, and Proven Winners.

Finally, throughout the evolution of this book, my own garden has served as a studio or a kind of laboratory where color experiments could be conducted, and this required the help of many hands over the years. In particular, I want to thank Wes Parsons, Chris Ison, and Bobby Cunningham for their reliable support; and my brother, Chris Smith, for his expertise and good sense of humor.

CONTENTS

CRACKING OPEN A NEW BOX OF CRAYONS

is often our first memory of the joy of choosing colors. I recall how a stack of paper and a pile of those waxy markers kept me occupied for hours. Delight surged through me as I hunted through the rainbow of hues to find just the right one. Long before the paper wrapper wore off, I had memorized each color by name: burnt sienna, spring green, mahogany, midnight blue, and cornflower were some of my favorites. As children, crayons were our first keys to unlocking the world of color as we scribbled and scrawled images of things around us.

My playmates seemed to lose interest in drawing pictures as the years went by, but I continued to be mesmerized by the activity, and I wanted to try out other ways of applying color to paper. Crayons gave way to finger paints, then tempera, and eventually watercolors and oil paints. Even today, one of the most relaxing things for me is to spend hours completely absorbed in painting a picture.

That's why *Colors for the Garden* is such a joy for me. As a garden designer, that same childhood thrill surges through me each time I "paint" with plants upon the canvas of a garden. Talk about the ultimate box of crayons! And through designing gardens I have found a way to merge my passions for plants and art into the practice of arranging both into an ever-changing landscape.

As I work in my chosen profession, it has become clear to me that selecting colors for a garden is more than just understanding color theories. Because nature and time are my creative partners in every design, gardens are not static but dynamic productions that unfold as the plants grow and the seasons turn. Long after the stage is set with all the plants, tables, chairs, and accessories, the color scheme continues to evolve. As the days go

Opposite: When we were young, experimenting to find which crayon best matched the color of our house, water, grass, and trees helped to imprint the color connections we still hold today.

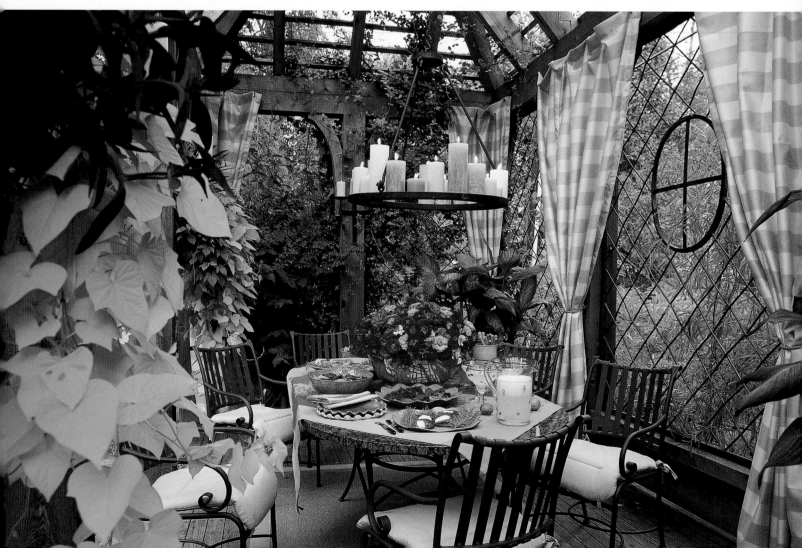

by, the plants assume new roles—some that began as supporting cast members mature into leads. The plant "actors" enter and exit the stage as they grow, bloom, subside, or don new seasonal colors. This vibrant transformation is what keeps me so enthralled with creating gardens year after year.

Now, I must admit that no matter how many times I develop a garden design, I often feel the same trepidation that many of my clients express when it comes to choosing a color palette. With the thousands of plants available and the myriad ways they can be combined, who wouldn't feel overwhelmed? That's why I wanted to write this book on color—to share the formulas, tips, and tricks I've discovered (often the hard way) that can help you confidently choose and apply colors in an outdoor setting.

Color is all about relationships. First and foremost, there is the relationship between color and light: for humans to be able to see the spectrum of colors, the object must be illuminated. That's why the quality of light is so important—be it dim or strong, it changes the way colors appear. Also, there is the relationship that colors have to each other. For instance, a patch of the same color of blue seems to change against background colors of yellow, or green, or orange. These relationships are true in painting and in gardening. However, where these activities seem to part ways is in the use of the color wheel.

To make the color wheel an effective tool for garden designs requires a bit of reinterpretation. While artists begin a painting with a canvas or blank slate, gardeners start with a canvas already full of existing elements, such as the house, driveway, fences, grass, trees, and shrubs. The dominant colors found in most of these components are variants of greens, along with shades of brown, black, white, and gray. These colors serve as the background or "neutral" canvas upon which the other hues in the color wheel can be applied. They are referred to as neutral, not because they are indistinct or inactive, but because they are usually the color constants in a garden's canvas. Once you remove these neutral colors from this spectrum, the remaining colors can be divided into two categories: cool (blue, pink, purple, magenta) and warm (red, orange, apricot, yellow). These three color groups—neutral, cool, and warm—provide the framework upon which this book is written. I offer it here as a way to gently unweave the complexities of color so you can relax and enjoy creating gardens that will excite and delight you.

To guide you through the process, the book is divided into three parts. Part One, "Choosing Colors for Your Garden," offers five different methods to select the colors that are best suited to your style and setting. Read through all five ideas and then use one or a combination of several of the methods to discover the perfect palette. Experience has taught me that the most memorable gardens are those that blend together a home's interior and exterior spaces into a single unit I call the "garden home." This concept encourages homeowners to divide their outdoor spaces into a series of rooms, much like they have inside their homes. By reinterpreting your interior rooms into outdoor settings, you can greatly expand your living space into more useable areas. And by connecting those spaces with harmonizing colors, the garden appears as a natural extension of the house, beautifying your home's exterior and improving the views from the inside.

Part Two, "Using Colors Creatively," provides tips on how to effectively apply colors in a garden setting. These techniques will guide your hand in placing colors within your landscape to give your garden a polished look.

Opposite, above left: This bright mixed border is sure to be the topic of conversation as visitors sit at the table to enjoy a cool drink. **Above right:** Painting is a relaxing outlet for me that I enjoy even more in an outdoor setting. **Below:** The jewel-tone palette chosen for this poolside cabana accentuates the relaxing and festive atmosphere of the site.

Throughout Parts One and Two, you'll also find activities and references to the principles of design described in my first book, *P. Allen Smith's Garden Home.* The principles are repeated here as a reminder of the many ways color and the elements of design are interwoven.

Part Three, "Color Expressions," is a resource guide to help you find plants expressing your garden's color themes. The guide is divided into the three color families described earlier: cool, warm, and neutral.

Cool Colors

Warm Colors

Neutral Colors

An introduction to each color group descibes the characteristics of that family and how the hues act to create moods, make areas appear larger or smaller, and either heat up or cool down the visual temperature of a garden. The plants listed in the color directories reflect those that I rely on in my garden designs for good color, vitality, ease of care, and dependability. Knowledgeable staff at local garden centers should also be familiar with these plants, and if they don't carry that exact variety, they can help you find alternative cultivars particularly well suited for your area. Garden club members or friends and family members with gardening experience can also be helpful. To explore more plant choices, visit my website, www.pallensmith.com.

My sincere hope is that the ideas and images found on these pages will inspire and encourage you to try your hand at painting a landscape full of your favorite colors. Once you've had the experience, I'm sure you will find there's nothing like the thrill of living in your own work of art.

Opposite: Take the "visual temperature" of the plants pictured here and see if you can name their color family. Do they belong to the cool, warm, or neutral group? Notice how the orange blooms of the 'Enchantment' lilies heat up the page while the lavender petals of 'Purple Dome' aster cool it down. The soft gray foliage of dusty miller falls somewhere in the middle. As a neutral color, gray mixes easily with both warm and cool hues.

Part One

CHOOSING
COLORS
FOR YOUR GARDEN

AS YOU START TO PONDER WHAT COLORS YOU'D LIKE TO USE IN YOUR GARDEN, I CAN ALMOST HEAR YOU SAY, "I don't have a clue how to begin." But you may be more of a color expert than you realize. Think back to this morning as you scanned your closet for something to wear. Although you may not have been fully awake, some part of your brain was probably thinking, "I want to put on this shirt, so I need to pick slacks that will go with those colors." Or, another time, you may have found yourself in a paint store staring at a sea of color chips about to choose wall

"All gardening is landscape painting."
—WILLIAM KENT

paint. To narrow the selection you may have brought in samples of colors from the rugs or curtains in that room. Many of the considerations you use when you are picking colors for your wardrobe or your home are the same ones that will guide you in choosing colors for your garden. The first step is to look at the color choices you've already made and use them to create connections to your outdoor settings. As you begin this process, there's really only one hard and fast "color rule": Choose colors you like. Who knows? You may be the one to set the next trend.

Our color preferences are influenced by the way a color speaks to us emotionally. For example, when seeking a tranquil lifestyle, many people are innately drawn to softer colors. Conversely, preferences for bright hues may reflect a desire for more stimulation. Personality can also play a role. Often, introverted people prefer quieter or deeper colors, while extroverts like an outgoing, vibrant palette. Climate can be a factor. If you live where summers are hot, cool garden colors may seem like a fresh breeze.

Whatever drives your preferences, my five strategies for choosing colors will help you put together a personalized color palette for your garden. Look through them all and then mix and match the ideas that best fit your setting.

Opposite, above: A clean and contemporary house calls for a similar outdoor setting. For a touch of contrast, flowing plumes of purple fountain grass in a cluster of containers soften the sleek lines of the furniture. When viewed from inside the house, this setting appears as a natural extension of the interior decor. **Below left:** Bright striped pillows in an outdoor sitting area can be seen from the window of this artist's studio. When the same colors are used in both realms, the line between inside and out disappears. **Below right:** A cool color combination of lavender 'Globe Master' allium, blue iris, and soft pink roses helps to foreshadow the color theme found inside the house.

Connect Colors Inside and Out

Only a gardener would think it was possible to transplant a 1905 Colonial Revival Cottage from one side of town to the other. At least that's what my friends told me when they saw my roofless, porchless shell of a house sitting forlornly on its new corner lot. Once the house arrived, I was so overwhelmed with all the things I needed to do both inside and out that when it came time to paint the interior rooms, I impulsively decided to cover them all with the same neutral wall color. "Cold Oatmeal" was the name most visitors gave to the color of my interior walls. While it wasn't very inspiring, it did buy me some time while I considered a livelier palette.

One of the first rooms I decided to repaint was my study. It had a set of large double windows that overlooked an area of the yard that I was transforming into a fountain garden. I wanted some privacy for this space from the street, so I planted the borders with needlepoint holly. When the day came to choose a color for the study, I was sitting in front of the windows looking outside into the garden. Suddenly, I was struck with the idea of using the deep green color of the hedge as the color for the walls. It seemed the perfect way to connect both spaces. The paint store salesman did a double take when I dug out a holly leaf from my pocket, held it up proudly and asked, "Can you match this color?" But once he saw I was serious, he mixed the perfect blend.

Later, as I developed color accents in the study, I brought those hues out into the garden, adding plants, containers, and furniture in related shades. The lesson I learned was that by allowing the colors inside and outside my home to echo each other, I created color connections between these adjoining spaces that established a cohesive feeling. The surprising result of this technique is that it enlarges the sense of space in both areas. Consider this technique in rooms that overlook your yard.

Another way to further define your color preferences is by playing off the attributes of your home's decor. Is it traditional, country, contemporary, or an eclectic mix? Each decorating approach suggests a certain array of associated colors. If your home is bold and modern then you may be leaning toward bright, strong, highly contrasting colors. On the other hand, if rustic or casual settings are more to your liking, traditional colors with a soft, weathered patina may reflect your color preferences.

The patterns used in your home's upholstery, draperies, rugs, accent pillows, and wallpaper also indicate your approach to color. If you are drawn to plaids, stripes, and checks, you may define visual comfort in terms of order, regularity, and neatness, whereas geometric patterns offer a sense of simplicity and structure. If florals are more to your liking, this may indicate a relaxed, informal side to your decorating personality. The colors expressed in these patterns can also help identify your preferred color combinations. Consider duplicating these color combinations and styles to outdoor settings. In some cases, textures, rather than patterns, may define your interior furnishings. In that situation, textural variety in plants and accessories would be equally important as color.

Now, this doesn't mean that you must use colors with equal intensity or in the same combination in each realm. A less dominant color in a room could serve as the leading hue in an outdoor color scheme. For example, if apricot is an accenting hue in an interior room

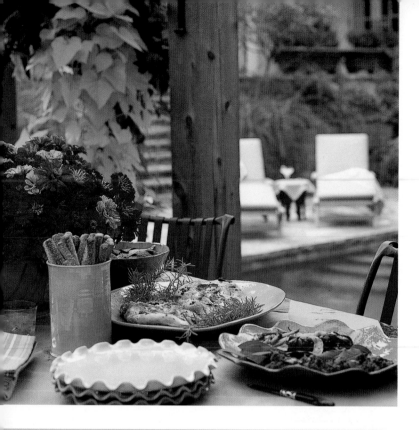

Preceding pages, left: A covered walkway between the house and garage is my favorite in-between room. Located outside the kitchen door and just a stone's throw from my vegetable garden, the area is the perfect spot to relax, pot up plants, or arrange a bouquet. The style of the room's furniture and its color palette reflect my interior decor. **Preceding pages, above right:** The sky-blue flowers of 'Imperial Blue' plumbago are illuminated against the richly hued foliage of Persian shield (*Strobilanthes*) and 'Plum Frost' coleus. **Preceding pages, below:** A freshly picked bucket of blooms is ready to be arranged for a spot of color indoors. **Left:** Home and garden color themes blend easily around this active backyard gathering spot. To match the spirit of the family's lively activities, an energetic mixture of rich golds and reds with splashes of cool blues and lime greens keeps the energy high but refreshed. **Below left:** Equally bold in hue and style to the outdoor setting above, this hot color combination of striped 'Tropicanna' canna leaves and 'Kiwi Fern' coleus fires things up.

activity

Gather paint chips, fabric swatches, and rug and flooring samples from various rooms to discover your interior color themes. Organize them into a scrapbook or journal along with inspiring photographs of favorite gardens and plants.

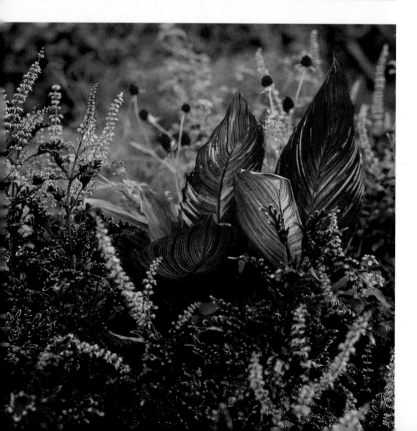

that is primarily decorated in a range of grays and sage greens, an apricot rose growing over an arbor just outside that room would create a beautiful connecting color, as well as an opportunity to make an arrangement of cut flowers to bring inside.

One of the great benefits of coordinating garden colors to your home's interior is that the plants you grow will be ideal for cutting and creating arrangements that match your decor. I have a friend whose interest in gardening began after she took a flower-arranging class. When she saw the magnificent bouquets that could be created, she wanted to use flowers from her own garden so her arrangements would be in just the right colors.

How much or how little you use of a color to blend indoor and outdoor spaces may depend on the view from a room's windows and doors. One family I worked with spent a lot of time in their family room, which had large French doors that overlooked a shady terrace. The room was light and airy, painted in cream with white trim. Through the windows you could see a brick wall that ran along the back of the property. To extend the feeling of the family room outside we planted a big bank of oak leaf hydrangeas along the brick wall. When the shrubs came into bloom, their large creamy white flowers matched the colors inside the family room, bringing the two areas together. We also placed large containers filled with light-colored caladiums just outside the doors of the family room on the terrace. These touches made the whole exterior feel connected to the view inside and created a most inviting setting. If the windows had been small with little view to the outside, the strong cream and white color echo may not have been as important.

| COLOR |

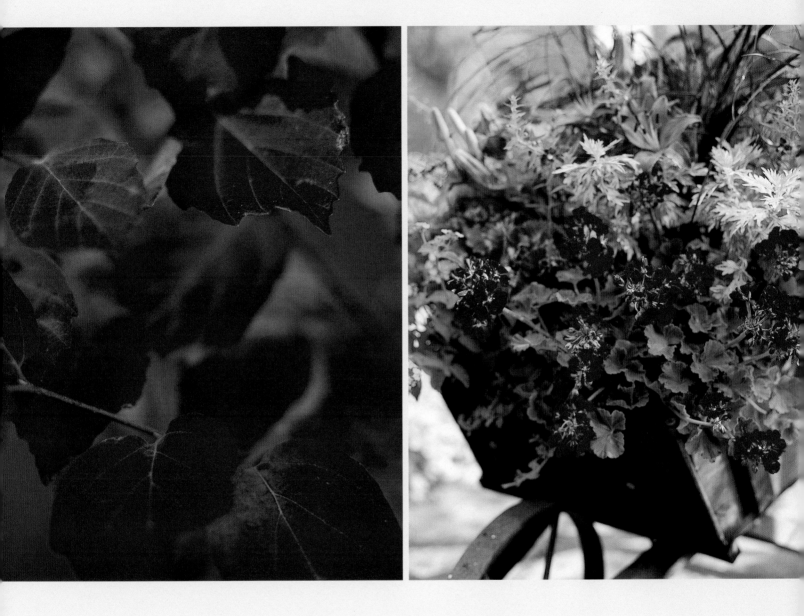

Drench your garden in color with bursts of blooms and floods of foliage. Just as a striking flower arrangement sets off a room, pools of color can enliven an outdoor setting. Look for color inspiration both inside and outside your home. The colors found in a favorite fabric can be reproduced in a collection of plants as with the wheelbarrow arrangement above, while an outside focal point such as this tree covered in brilliant red fall leaves may serve as a color connection to red accents in a nearby room. When you apply color-coordinating hues, house and garden blend together into a unified whole, enhancing the beauty of both. Harness the power of the spectrum by using its mood-altering effects to your advantage. Create calm, spacious feelings with cool colors such as blue, lavender, pink, purple, and magenta. Or heighten the drama and bring areas of the garden forward with yellow, orange, apricot, and red. Whatever palette you choose, splash on the color in a bold way.

Reveal or Conceal Your Home

There is one lesson that has been so valuable to me that I have it chiseled into a stepping-stone just outside my door. It is Alexander Pope's missive to "consult the genius of the place in all." I have found that when I look closely, every landscape has admirable qualities. And when those unique characteristics are recognized and enhanced, a property evolves beyond the standard cookie-cutter design to become a distinctive and memorable garden home.

You can unlock the genius of your place and discover its signature colors by examining your property with an eye toward its best features. Tap into this element of your home's character by studying its architectural style. Since the house is the largest object in the landscape, it is important to come to terms with the building. Like the pink elephant in the middle of the room that everyone sees but no one mentions, you need to acknowledge the impact of your home's exterior design on the garden and determine if it is something to emphasize or play down.

If the architecture of the house is strong, let it lead. Take its best features and bring them into the garden. If you find the structural design doesn't warrant being emphasized, you have three basic choices: repaint it, cover it up, or direct the eye away from the house. As Frank Lloyd Wright once said, "A doctor can bury his mistakes, but an architect can only advise his clients to plant vines."

If you choose to let it lead, then allow your home's design to guide your color choice in the garden. For example, contemporary homes suggest the use of bold primary colors, just as a softer, pastel palette is better suited for a Victorian house.

While modern homes are rarely exact replicas of historical designs, they often reflect elements of the past that give clues to their architectural roots. For example, a flared roofline, shingled walls, prominent overhang, porch columns supported on stone, and a fieldstone chimney are all features found on bungalow-style houses. Similar features may be present in new construction reminiscent of this architectural style. Examine your home for signs of its architectural influences and then select a color that reflects that style. The colors you might choose for a Santa Fe house wouldn't feel quite right on a Georgian or Federal-style home. Color palettes found in Colonial Williamsburg would be a better match. Likewise, warm Mediterranean colors would enhance the architecture of an Italianate home.

To play down the focus on your home, use exterior colors such as cream, tan, gray, and white. These hues allow for more flexibility in developing a garden palette because they don't fight or clash with either warm or cool colors. I painted my own home a medium gray for that reason. It provides a harmonious background that allows me to develop nearly any color scheme I desire.

One of the more challenging house colors to design around is red or terra-cotta brick. During the 1950s and 1960s a great number of houses were built with this material. Since it is such a strong and warm color, you have to be careful in selecting a palette of hues that creates a harmonious blend. When I am faced with this challenge, I usually recommend one of two choices: either work with the color or conceal it.

For example, one of my clients purchased a salmon-color brick house and they wanted to know what they could do to help soften its impact in the landscape. Since it was a good

COLONIAL TRADITIONAL

Bungalow

Victorian

Mediterranean

Modern

Opposite: Coordinating the garden's colors with the exterior of the house creates a pleasing effect. Distinctive architectural designs often look best with particular varieties of plants. The tall Italian cypress and the pink and white rose-drenched landscape complement this Italianate-style home. In other examples, you would expect to find vine-covered arbors, peonies, and hollyhocks growing around a cottage, whereas palm trees and bougainvillea are more the norm for a Floridian coastal home.

Above: Succulent plants, such as those pictured here, are good candidates for an adobe-style home. Their thick, leathery leaves make them well suited for dry, harsh conditions. **Above right:** This New England saltbox-style garden reflects the historical roots of the home. In the past, a fenced and gated area surrounding the house was necessary to protect valued flowers and vegetables from livestock and wildlife. Today, the enclosed garden creates a quiet enclave. **Right:** The beautiful weathered exterior of this New England saltbox home offers a backdrop of neutral color to display a soft palette of flowers. **Opposite, above:** The light brown exterior of this adobe-style home matches the colors of the driveway and stone terrace that surround it, giving the house the appearance that it grew out of the earth. **Below far left:** This cool-themed mixed border in my garden is packed with plants. Deep, generous beds with an abundance of shrubs, perennials, and annuals are classic qualities found in cottage gardens. **Below left:** Lavender and cream flowers fill the borders of the walkway leading to the raised terrace.

activity

Photograph the exterior of your home and garden. When you do, you'll find a very curious thing happens: The areas around your home take on a different appearance. By framing the view through the lens and in pictures, the shapes of plants, buildings, and objects become more apparent. Also, items that create visual clutter—such as garbage cans, power lines, or the neighbor's utility shed—suddenly stand out. Use the photographs to create or improve the garden settings around your home.

architectural example of a fifties-style house, it didn't seem appropriate to paint the brick. So we developed a palette of plants to tone down the terra-cotta color: primarily white, lavender, and purple with accents of salmon and apricot and a sprinkling of blue-gray foliage.

Along with the house, identify other large elements of existing color on your property, such as the garage and other outbuildings, fences, terraces, decks, and walkways. Decide if you want to highlight them by bringing the colors into other parts of the garden or if you want to conceal these features by repainting them with an inconspicuous color, covering them with vines, or screening them from view.

Above: Good garden design is really about creating beautiful scenes. To help you identify your best settings, use a simple viewfinder such as a picture mat. Hold it up and isolate a particular object or scene to find the best composition. By eliminating surrounding distractions, it is easier to orchestrate good color combinations. **Left:** Open gates beckon visitors up the winding stone pathway past a cool spray of Spanish lavender to the rose-covered entrance. The colors in the garden echo the soft gold exterior of the home and the gray limestone accenting the doorway. **Opposite, above:** Azaleas loaded with white lacy blooms fill the flowerbeds along this walkway. The home's light-colored exterior is extended into the landscape with the help of these beautiful shrubs. **Opposite, below:** The white pillars supporting the archway to my fountain garden are the same color and design as those on my front porch. Repeating the house's architectural features in the garden strengthens the connection between the two areas. Large pots of white tulips continue the white theme.

| SHAPE AND FORM |

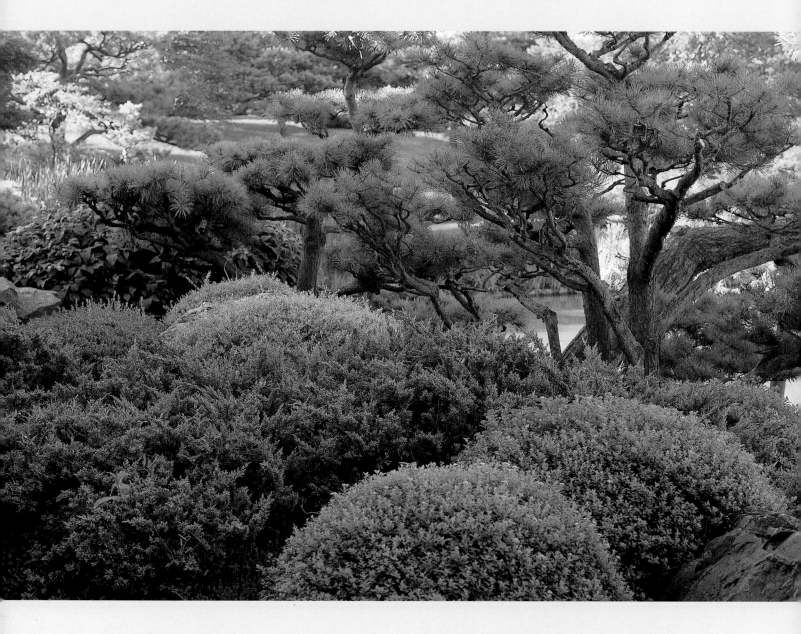

The shape and form of plants, along with their color, contribute to your garden's personality. For instance, while most trees are variants of green, their distinctive shapes add to their style of expression. Upright, linear, and erect plant forms give a garden a lift and a sense of formality, while weeping, spreading, and fountainesque shapes create a more relaxed and casual space. By recognizing the personalities that are often linked with each plant form, you can create plant combinations to express the style you have in mind. Combining color and form allows you to play up or down the quality associated with each shape. For example, the mounded forms of the evergreen trees and shrubs pictured here echo the rounded stones and rolling green hillside. Imagine the same area covered in tall, conical spruce trees with bright pockets of blooming forsythia. Splashes of yellow amid the vertical green forms would give the garden a much different feel.

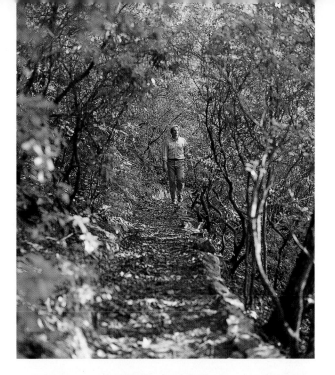

Play Off Nature's Palette

As you walk or drive through your neighborhood and other nearby areas, notice the colors in the surrounding landscape. Natural features, such as rock outcroppings, lakes, waterways, and vegetation, can provide inspirations for your color choices.

A homeowner who moved into an older, established neighborhood was trying to select a color to paint his house and decided to take a stroll around the block to become better acquainted with the area. As he ambled along the shady avenue past his home, he noticed soft green lichen growing on the north side of the trees. The color had great appeal to him, so he decided to take a sample into the local home-improvement store and have a house paint blended to match the color. When the paint had dried, his home was completely transformed and looked as though it had grown out of the landscape. The color echoed an indigenous hue, making his house fit comfortably in its setting.

Some homeowners are fortunate to live in or nearby natural areas. Woodlands, prairies, deserts, rivers and lakes as well as wetlands or mountains all exhibit their own unique color qualities that come from the area's geology and native vegetation. Architects, sensitive to these environmental distinctions, create homes and other buildings that reflect the spirit of the area's natural expression. Adobe-style homes and xeriscape gardens of the arid Southwest capture the colors found in the surrounding desert and mountains. In Maine, shingled gray houses look natural amid the granite rocks and pine trees, and the red barns that dot the landscape provide a stark contrast. No matter where you live, nature always adorns the land in an artful spectrum of colors. When you select a color theme that harmonizes with the regional landscape, your home and garden will seem more grounded to the setting.

Seasonal changes in your region may also influence your color selections. When you have spectacular color cycles in the landscape, you can embrace them and bring them closer to your home. I planted two 'Red Sunset' maples (*Acer rubrum*) in front of my house to create a "Kodak moment" when the leaves turn fire-engine red each autumn. A short-lived burst of color like a glorious fall tree or a spring-flowering shrub heralds a new season and can be as satisfying as a plant that provides a full season of color.

In small spaces, large seasonal plants and trees can dominate the area and influence your garden's color palette throughout the year. In my oval-shaped rondel garden, the canopies of four 'Narragansett' crabapples knit together to

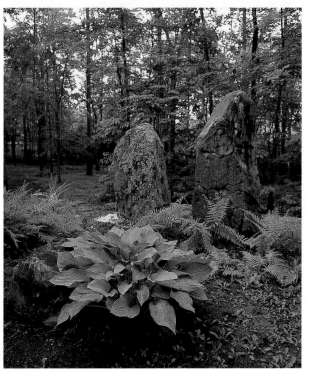

Top: Stroll through a nearby natural area to find inspiration. By borrowing colors from the local landscape, your garden will appear anchored to the setting. **Above:** The glaucous leaves of 'Krossa Regal' hosta pick up the colors in the weathered, upright gray stones. The plant helps to signal a bend in the path.

form a ceiling over the area. When their spring blossoms open, the garden is crowned in a halo of pink flowers. In the fall, the dark green leaves turn bronze, and throughout winter, the trees are adorned in red berries. These seasonal hues are so striking they act as the color inspirations for that area. If you have a small garden and want to play off a plant's cyclical color change, look for one that offers interest year-round, with flowers in the spring or summer, colorful foliage in the fall, and interesting bark or fruit sets in the winter.

Above: Following nature's lead, moss was encouraged to grow in this shady area of the landscape, creating a magical terraced garden of soft, spongy greens. **Above right:** The forms of these weeping willow trees signal both strength and flexibility. Their thick trunks and branches appear powerful while their long, sweeping branches are thin and wispy. The narrow green leaves serve as a cool canopy of shade. Recognizing how color works with plant shapes to define a garden's personality enables you to create just the right atmosphere. **Above far right:** A plant's form as well as its color gives a garden expression. This tall, somewhat unruly verbena-on-a-stick (*Verbena bonariensis*) lends a wild and spontaneous quality to the flower border. **Below right:** Wide swaths of colors echoing those from the surrounding landscape give this carefully designed meadow above a lake the happenstance look of nature's handiwork. **Below far right:** Large, uneven slabs of stone appear as though they were haphazardly laid down, supplying the garden with a natural, spontaneous feel. This quality is enhanced by the way the plantings are arranged in clusters or colonies, much as you find them in nature.

activity

Gather flowers from your garden or nearby areas for bouquets to help you explore the regional color palettes. Use this as an opportunity to experiment with the colors and textures to see how they work with the established elements of your garden, such as the color of your house, the soil, or even a fence. Understanding which plants perform reliably in your area will help you create a strong foundation and will increase the likelihood of pleasing results.

| FOCAL POINT |

Transform your garden with a visual hook. It seems to be part of our nature to look around for something to grab our attention when we enter a new place. Once we see something that piques our interest, our focus goes to that point and the rest of the room falls into place. Color is an effective way to create a focal point. Altering the color of an object using a shocking hue is always an immediate attention-getter. Or place a colorful object at the end of a "runway," such as a path or parallel lines of trees and shrubs, to direct the eye. For a more subtle approach, choose a focal point in a harmonizing color, such as the weathered gray bench pictured here. Notice how it blends with the silver, white, and glaucous plants in this gray garden, but its hard shape makes it stand out from the feathery forms of the plants surrounding it.

Feature a Favorite

If you find yourself overwhelmed with the kaleidoscope of color choices, simplify the process by focusing on one element in your garden to use as a starting point. This could be a colorful piece of patio furniture, a container, or even a favorite plant. The most effective color themes spring from a dominant color that anchors the design. By choosing one key color from an object or plant as inspiration, you are less likely to add other colors that quarrel with the theme.

A colorful foliage plant that I like is 'Tilt-a-Whirl' coleus. The plant is aptly named for the way its chocolaty peach leaves with chartreuse highlights appear to whirl around the stem. By taking one leaf from this plant and carefully looking at its colors, you can build an entire color scheme. Start by focusing on the chartreuse veining and then looking for plants to echo that color. One successful combination I've found is mixing 'Tilt-a-Whirl' coleus with creeping Jenny and 'Evergold' sedge. The lime green in creeping Jenny's foliage and the yellow tones in the 'Evergold' sedge pick up the chartreuse highlights in the 'Tilt-a-Whirl' leaves.

As gardeners, we would all be better served to remember the importance of foliage when considering plant combinations—whether it is for a large garden scheme, a small garden room, or even an ensemble of plants in a single container. However, this is often easier

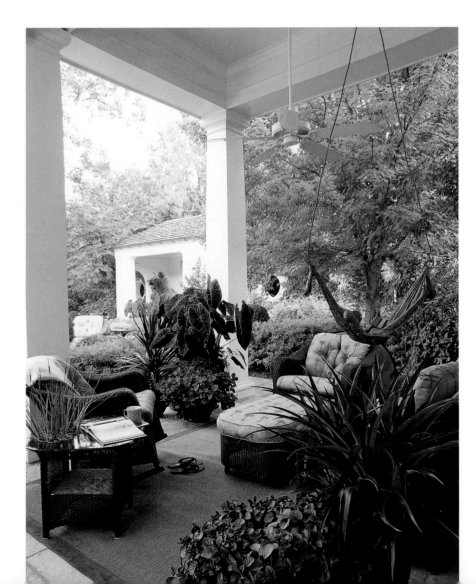

Above: The homeowners' collection of bronze statues served as the color inspiration for the patio pictured below. Two boys happily at play set the mood for a relaxed garden setting. **Left:** To complement the bronze color of the statues, black wicker furniture and pots of tropical plants with dark foliage were added. The deep saturated colors give this outdoor room visual weight. Thick, comfortable cushions covered in taupe fabric invite visitors to sit down and stay awhile. The taupe color harmonizes with the sisal rug and stone flooring. A variety of textures and forms gives the setting visual interest and helps to set the room apart from the landscape just beyond.

activity

Visit a local garden center or nursery with an eye focused on colorful foliage plants. Some full-sun foliage plants to look for are Persian shield, coleus, 'Tropicanna' canna, perilla, and variegated sweet potato vine. Bring along paint chips, fabric swatches, and samples of floor coverings from your outdoor settings. Compare the samples with the foliage to find plants that will enhance your decor. Make sure the plants are well suited for the light and water conditions in which they will be growing.

said than done. Even for the trained eye, it is the bloom of a plant that captures our attention. But when you think about it, flowers are often temporary, blooming for a few days and then gone. Kevin Doyle said it best: "Texture and foliage keep a garden interesting through the season. Flowers are just moments of gratification." You'll enjoy a longer lasting display of color by incorporating foliage plants into your designs.

Next time you go to a garden center, try this exercise: First, choose one dominant color for your garden plan and then select a representative flower (preferably something that has a long blooming cycle) in that color. Next, find a foliage plant that is a good color companion and put them together. With these two plants chosen, add another blooming plant and see how this looks with its companions.

By looking at plants this way, you will begin to see more possibilities. When you look past the flower, you begin to notice the color and pattern of the plant's foliage. An even closer inspection reveals more colors on the underside of the leaves and perhaps interesting stems or bark. A full inventory of a plant's characteristics gives you a wider range of design applications, adding more layers of sophistication to your color combinations.

Another starting point for building a color scheme is to use a favorite paint color. Paint a board with the color you have in mind and then place various flowers and foliage samples

Above left: Deep burgundy 'Negrita' tulips emerge from a bed of purple violas against a striking backdrop of sweet iris (*Iris pallida* 'Aureo Variegata'). In early spring the spear-shaped foliage of the variegated iris begins nearly lemon yellow, and then fades to creamy white through the summer, allowing you to choreograph an evolving palette of colors around the plant. **Below left:** Do you love the color purple? Although each container is filled with a different plant, clustering them together makes a compelling combination. The sultry color of 'Midnight Train' coleus is repeated in the throat of the petunia. To keep the arrangement from getting too moody, 'Silver Spike' helichrysum brightens the scene. **Opposite, above left:** An engaging mix of flowers and foliage keeps this hot-color border from burning up the garden. A variety of foliage plants, including 'Kiwi Fern' and 'Copper' coleus along with Persian shield and 'Purple Heart' setcreasea, adds long-lasting color without fanning the flames of the fiery blooms. **Opposite, right:** An easy way to color-coordinate your flower borders is to start with a favorite plant, such as the multi-hued 'Tropicanna' canna, and then find other plants that go with it. Here I'm holding a stem of *Salvia vanhouttei* 'Paul' next to the canna. It looks like a perfect match. **Opposite, below left:** To punch up the color excitement in a flower border, toss in the swirling foliage of 'Tilt-a-Whirl' coleus. Combine it with the striped leaves and orange blooms of 'Tropicanna' canna, and you'll really get the party going!

Here are some examples of foliage and flower combinations for a sunny location that will provide lasting color all summer long.

EXAMPLE 1: FIRE AND ICE

NAME	TYPE	COLOR	COLOR CATEGORY
Sweet potato 'Margarita'	Foliage	Brilliant chartreuse	Neutral
Golden lantana	Bloom	Rich yellow	Warm
Scaevola 'Blue Jam'	Bloom	Purple	Cool

EXAMPLE 2: RARE GEM

NAME	TYPE	COLOR	COLOR CATEGORY
Purple heart/setacreasea	Foliage	Plum	Neutral
Copper plant/acalypha	Foliage	Bronze/salmon variegated	Warm
Pink pentas	Bloom	Medium pink	Cool

EXAMPLE 3: TICKLE ME PINK

NAME	TYPE	COLOR	COLOR CATEGORY
Coleus 'Touch of Class'	Foliage	Chartreuse	Neutral
Mandevilla/pink	Bloom	Medium pink	Cool
Pink penta	Bloom	Medium pink	Cool

EXAMPLE 4: TROPICAL TWIST

NAME	TYPE	COLOR	COLOR CATEGORY
Canna 'Tropicanna'	Foliage	Salmon/green variegated	Warm
Coleus 'Tilt-a-Whirl'	Foliage	Orange variegated	Warm
Salvia vanhouttei 'Paul'	Bloom	Purple mauve	Cool

against the board to see which combinations you like. While you may not choose to paint your home these colors, the hues could represent the color of a tablecloth, chair pads, containers, or accent pillows in your garden room.

The painted boards and plants also serve as a reminder that colors in the garden are represented in both living and inert objects. Each responds differently to light, but when they are combined to create the decor of a garden, the composition takes on an engaging appearance. You can observe this for yourself by placing a painted object, such as a chair or bench, next to a planted container. The quality of colors in the plants has a lively spirit and energy that isn't visible in inert materials. The brilliance and profusion of nature's colors comes from the organic pigments in the plants. Paints, on the other hand, are created from synthetic pigments, so they display a different character. When you play one dimension off of the other, the visual interest is heightened in both.

Other kinds of inert objects can also serve as points of departure for a color palette, such as a sculpture, building, fountain, bench, or other outstanding features in a garden room. The white columns, railing, and trim on my front porch stand out as its strongest architectural features, so as I was selecting foundation plants, I decided a white rose, 'Madame Plantier', would help extend the color of those features into the garden. I picked up the theme by placing a white urn in the border. This made a more effective color connection to the porch than if I had selected a rose with a red bloom.

As summer progresses, the white theme drifts deeper into the border with other flowering plants such as phlox 'David' and a white buddleia. To extend this color and architectural echo elsewhere in the garden, I positioned an arbor to my fountain garden with white columns similar to those on the porch. Another white rose, 'Frau Karl Druschki', covers the bonnet of the arbor, strengthening the color connection to the house. Whether it is fabric, furniture, paint, or a plant, by choosing a single color from a favorite feature, you can create a solid foundation for a successful color theme in your garden.

Above and below left: Understanding how colors are affected by surrounding or adjacent colors is important in garden design. Imagine the yellow flowers placed against a yellow background; they would all but disappear for lack of contrast. Notice how the intensity of the hues also comes into play. While the flowers in the top picture are all shades of yellow, the ones closest to the same depth of color as the background stand out less than those on either end.

| ABUNDANCE |

The word "abundance" captures the very essence of a garden. Growing a bounty of food and flowers defines the reason we love to garden. Color plays an important role in building the sense of profusion by helping the eye to define the type and volume of various groups of plants. By following nature's lead and planting in large colonies and drifts of colors, your garden will appear spontaneous, natural, and full. Relaxed plantings in groupings of three, five, or seven, or large patches of color seem more pleasing than strict lines of plants. Abundant areas of color also ensure that you will have enough blooms to pick and use in the house without ruining the effect of the display. One thing to keep in mind as you fill your borders with color is to make sure you know where abundance ends and excess begins. If a single element overshadows all others in a composition, then it is time to rein it in to keep it in balance.

Embrace New Possibilities

While there are several ways to find the right colors for your garden, sometimes the best source of inspiration comes along by chance. One day, my brother dropped by to help me with a project. As he was unloading the supplies, he pushed in a bright red wheelbarrow and parked it in my rondel garden. With other thoughts on my mind as I walked into the area, the wheelbarrow's bold flash of color caught me off guard and stopped me right in my tracks. The flowerbeds in that area were filled with soft, cool colors, so the wheelbarrow stood out like a sore thumb. But the surprising blaze of color ignited a spark of inspiration. I knew the time had come to shake up the colors in that border by tapping in to my extroverted side. Undaunted by my previous failed attempts at creating a satisfying composition of hot colors, I decided to try again. This time, I finally got it right. I've found that gardening is less about getting it perfect and more about having fun.

If you've always played it color safe, why not be a little daring and try something you've never tried before. Your experiments don't have to be costly or time consuming. Try a few new plants in a container or a cluster of pots as a way to test a new color combination. Noted English gardener Vita Sackville-West was known to carry a branch of a flowering plant around the garden until she found a place where it was most appealing. In that way she decided either to leave the plant where it was or move it to a new, more desirable location. You can do the same with several pots of experimental color combinations; try them in various locations until you find the place where they look best.

Another way to shake up your garden's status quo is to visit public or private gardens. They can be treasure troves of fresh and inspiring ideas for new color combinations. (For a list of some of the best gardens, refer to the back section of my first book, *P. Allen Smith's Garden Home.*)

During recent trips to Mexico and Florida, I became more aware of the enchantment of tropical plants. I saw beautiful gardens filled with banana trees, giant elephant ears, and bold drifts of cannas, so when I returned home, I looked for new opportunities to incorporate the varieties into my garden. Here are some easy ways to blend these bold and colorful plants into containers and borders:

- *Create a tropical corner on your patio — and accent the plants with bright fabrics, paint, and accessories.*
- *Cluster containers of tropicals together.*
- *Plant them directly in your beds or place containers of them as accents in your flower borders. Cordylines and cannas are ideal in large pots, adding vertical height and foliage color to summer compositions.*

These plants add an exotic and unexpected feel to sedate gardens. Because they are so easy to find and so reasonably priced I use them freely when I want to rev up the excitement in an area of my garden. Their tropical nature strikes a relaxed and casual tone, setting a lighthearted festive mood. While we may associate them with certain styles of homes, such as Mediterranean, Caribbean, Louisiana raised cottage, or Florida contemporary, I find that even with traditional architecture they can add flare and whimsy to summer planting schemes.

Opposite, above left: The delight of discovery is found in a child's excitement as she holds up a petal. Gardening is an ongoing adventure when we stay open to new ideas. **Above right:** A riotous explosion of hot colors erupts from the flower border in my garden. While I usually favor a calmer palette of cool hues, I decided to take on the challenge of exploring these extroverted colors. **Below left:** Tropical plants such as this white-veined 'Frydek' alocasia add an exotic flair to a window box of pink and red impatiens. **Below right:** Experiment with imaginative blends of patterns and color in containers to test daring new plant combinations. Here 'Miss Muffet' caladium accents an arrangement of red impatiens, 'Show and Tell' coleus, purple heart, the waxy green leaves of begonias, and strands of lime-green creeping Jenny.

| WHIMSY |

Stamp your garden with elements of surprise and delight to give it a lighthearted quality that is uniquely your own. Whether it is an unexpected scarecrow, an unusual plant, or a whimsical statue, incorporating a touch of fancy reminds us that gardens are fun. Colors can help set the stage by introducing hues in surprising ways. Instead of removing a dead tree, why not leave the trunk and branches and paint it a bright color? Polka dots on flowerpots and a bright yellow door on a garden shed are other ways to convey a playful feeling. Color can also help camouflage a surprise. The frogs pictured here blend in so well with the water that visitors must look twice to see that they are not real. Using colors in both ways helps to build layers of enchantment in a garden, some easy to see, others more hidden.

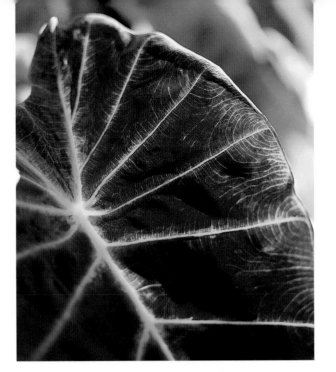

But you don't have to travel far from home to find inspiring new ideas. Look for planting demonstrations at local garden centers. Many nurseries create striking displays designed with plant materials from their inventories. Or, check out your local flower and garden shows; they feature exhibits and lectures by gardening experts. Even public areas, such as parks, shopping centers, and golf courses have large flowerbeds with plants selected to provide big color for extended periods of time. While the scale of the plantings may be quite different from your garden, you can pick up some ideas for new color combinations and see which plants are the most reliable performers.

Gather all your ideas in a journal or make a scrapbook of photos from garden magazines, books, even mail-order cata-

Colorful Tropical Plants

Hawaiian ti

Croton

Dracena

Cordyline

Canna

Elephant ears

Banana

Hibiscus

Variegated scheffelera

Oleander

Ginger

Bird of paradise

Ixora

Helyconia

Bromeliad varieties

Caladium

Calla lily

Palm

Variegated pineapple plant

Above: The dramatic black leaves and green veins of *Colocasia* 'Illustris' add an exotic flair to any setting. **Left:** *C.* 'Illustris' combines with 'Red Sensation' cordyline and *Plectranthus purpurea* to create a striking all-foliage container display.

logs. Some plant catalogs do an exceptional job of providing lyrical descriptions and stunning photographs of the plants they offer. By organizing all your information, you'll have it at your fingertips when you are ready to make your plans and go shopping.

Embracing new possibilities also means accepting and learning from our gardening mistakes. One year, I was on a mission to experiment with burgundy, purple, and black tulips. Whenever I try out new plant compositions I often use one of the raised beds in my vegetable garden. These 4 x 4-foot blocks are the perfect test plot size to serve as miniature canvases. In the fall, the bulbs arrived and were planted as planned. Later in the season, I found myself with some left-over yellow pansies and violas and was looking for a place to put them. The raised bed with the tulips appeared empty, so I stuck them there—having completely forgotten about the bulbs. What resulted was certainly not what I had originally planned, but once the dark tulips emerged amid the bright pansies and violas there was something about the combination that was daring and adventurous. At first, I saw the composi-tion as a mistake, but as garden visitors reacted positively to the unusual color combination, I began to see it through their eyes and appreciated its beauty.

Gardens are dynamic places. Don't be afraid to explore your adventuresome spirit. By allowing yourself to have fun and try some of these ideas, you are sure to discover the colors that speak to you.

Right: I enjoy experimenting with new formulas of color in the raised beds of my vegetable garden. These yellow violas were planted in the spring; af-terward, I remembered the bed had been already filled with tulip bulbs in various shades of lavender, purple, and magenta. This unplanned palette of colors was a pleasant surprise. **Opposite, above:** One of my major sources of inspiration is the magnificent garden at Arley Hall in Cheshire, England. As a young garden history student, my view of design was influ-enced by touring the finest gardens in Great Britain. **Opposite, below:** Many equally inspirational gardens can be found in the United States, such as the Chicago Botanic Garden, which offers all kinds of fresh and creative ideas that can be translated to landscapes of any size.

activity

Make a resolution to visit at least three new gardens this year. Take along a camera or your journal and document what you like and don't like about each one. Compare these characteristics to your own garden to spark your own creations.

Part Two

USING
COLORS
CREATIVELY

BY FOLLOWING THE TIPS IN PART ONE, YOU SHOULD NOW HAVE A GOOD IDEA OF THE COLORS YOU'D LIKE TO USE IN your garden. Now you are ready for a few quick lessons on how to "paint" those colors into your landscape. As you begin this process it helps to think of yourself, as Thomas Eakins suggests, as a "big artist." Many of the techniques used by the legendary painters translate to the garden and provide valuable tools to help you create your own masterpiece.

"The big artist keeps an eye on nature and steals her tools."
—THOMAS EAKINS

One of the first crossover principles that I have taken from painting and applied to gardening is to narrow the selections in each garden room to one color theme. When each outdoor setting has its own palette of hues, the character and style of different areas can be fully defined. If you have too many colors competing in a setting, the area feels disjointed.

Another art-to-garden lesson is to first establish main areas of color and then add the details. This approach avoids the pitfall of planting bits and dots of color so the eye has nowhere to land. Broad sweeps of color add an emotional charge and energy to a garden design.

When it comes to gathering colors for your landscape, it's easy to fall prey to the dazzling array of flowers that fill garden centers and nurseries in early spring. Just as choosing a color theme helps you organize the purchases inside your home, using a co-ordinated set of garden colors will save you time and money outside.

But before you head for the garden center, acquaint yourself with some basic design techniques that will help you set the stage for your colors.

Create a Canvas

An often overlooked but vital element in garden design is to create a backdrop on which to display your colors. There are three important reasons to add this component to your garden.

First, when a flowerbed is planted against a jumble of contrasting materials or colors, the composition gets lost in the clutter. A uniform backdrop creates a canvas so your eye is not distracted from seeing the colorful flowers and foliage in front of it. Typical garden canvases are a hedge, a line of small trees, a wall, a fence, the side of a building such as the house or garage, or an arbor or trellis. These canvases can be used individually or combined, such as a fence with a border of shrubs.

Another reason to add these backdrops is to help you create distinct outdoor living areas within your yard. Many homes sit in the middle of the property amid a sea of grass, encircled with the standard foundation plantings. In these cases, the only canvas available is the house and shrubbery. To create more opportunities for stunning floral displays, place canvases around the perimeter of the property, or section the yard into areas with defined purposes, such as dining, meditating, vegetable gardening, bird watching, or entertaining.

Ease of maintenance is another reason to establish background borders. Study any well-designed flower border and you'll discover that, more often than not, it is composed of three main components. 1. Structural plants: Shrubs, trees, roses, hedges that are the mainstay of the borders providing twelve months of interest, usually the backdrop of the border; 2. Supportive plants: Perennials, grasses, biennials, and bulbs that return each year and provide five to seven months of interest, often the middle of the border; 3. Temporary plants: Annuals, tropicals, and some bulbs that are present only during one growing season, usually in the foreground of the border.

Each element plays a role in creating the look of the garden throughout the year. The structural plants define the boundaries of a space much like the walls in your home. The supportive plants come back year after year without replanting, but die back through the winter months. The temporary plants are there for just one growing season and have to be added to the garden each spring. By establishing a solid canvas of structural plants and then filling in much of the remaining border with groupings of perennial supportive plants, the only areas that require replanting are the pockets of annual color. In my garden designs I purposely carve out coves within the borders that serve as seasonal flourishes of color, harmonizing with the more permanent members of the cast.

By thinking of your garden in this way, you can determine, based on your time and interests, how much of your borders you want to replant each year. If time is at a premium, but you still want to express yourself creatively, you can accomplish this by using more structural and supportive plants and reducing the areas of temporary annual plants.

The first year in my garden, I wanted plenty of immediate color so I planted lots of annuals. By the end of that first growing season, I knew I didn't want to go to all that work each year. So I made plans that fall to start planting a mixed border that would provide longstanding color and interest. I deepened the bed so I had space at the back to add the shrubs and small trees that would provide a textural background. Purple smoke tree, barberry, butterfly bush, old-fashioned shrub roses, elaeagnus, and variegated red twig dogwood provided maximum visual interest with a minimum of effort.

Opposite, above left: A variety of backdrops are illustrated in this setting: the walls of the house provide a canvas for vines and trees, a low stone wall serves as a division between spaces, and a patterned floor is formed by the boxwood and begonia planting. **Above right:** In a wave of white, sprays of bridal wreath spiraea blooms spill over the wall. **Center:** Crisp, precisely clipped boxwood hedges planted in a geometric pattern create an intriguing study in green. **Below left:** Mother Nature wipes the slate clean in my fountain garden with a fresh layer of snow. Winter scenes like this allow me to study the "bones," or framework, of each area without the distraction of summer colors. **Below right:** Structures such as fences, gates, posts, and benches serve as backdrops for compositions of color.

activity

Take an inventory of the canvases already in place in your garden. Look for solid backgrounds uniform in color and material, such as fences, hedges, trellises, arbors, or sides of buildings. Even sidewalks and pathways can be considered a type of canvas: you can add colorful plants along the side or in between stepping stones.

The structural backdrop plants within a border can be designed to have either a formal or informal feel, depending on the style of the garden. Formal gardens are generally based on ordered patterns and symmetrical designs. Crisp, straight-line plantings of a single variety of shrub establish a formal style, particularly if the foliage is fine leafed and clipped into strict geometric forms such as rectangles or ball shapes. A loose, mixed border of various trees and shrubs with a range of different leaf shapes and sizes, but uniform in color throughout the summer, has a more informal feel. The interaction between these opposites creates a visual tension that animates the design.

When selecting plants for the canvas, consider how they will look in all four seasons. To make sure that the border doesn't disappear when the plants lose their leaves in winter, consider evergreens as the outer band of the framework. While some might see an evergreen border as a bit too formal, I've found a touch of formality isn't something to be avoided and is especially effective in holding together more casual, unstructured plantings of perennials and annuals.

In certain situations, privacy, personal taste, or special site conditions might require a fence, wall, or building rather than planted borders. If you want your garden home to have an easy feel that fits comfortably with its environment, adopt elements from the house or local palette to express the building materials for these types of garden canvases. In the most harmonious settings, the color of brick and stone should feel as though it originated from the area. Native stone is always a good choice. When planting around building elements, you can add a layer of structural plants to soften the effect of the constructed material, or if you prefer, use the wall or fence itself as the canvas and add supportive and temporary plants in the foreground.

Opposite, above left: Uniform plantings of shrubs, such as these clipped boxwood parterres, make ideal canvases. Notice how the white tulips pop against the green foliage. **Left:** A dog-eared picket fence outlines the perimeter of my property and provides a consistent background element for a variety of plant compositions. Here snowball viburnums hang like white lanterns over the happy faces of 'Accent' daffodils and a cluster of boxwood shrubs. **Below left:** 'New Dawn' roses recline along the top of a low stone wall in this relaxing garden room. The stones in the wall echo the exterior of the house, creating a color bond.

| ENCLOSURE |

Establishing distinct garden spaces around your home is the secret to creating a garden home. As you section your yard into a series of defined areas, you are in effect unfolding the pattern of your home outside. This method unifies the areas inside and out and anchors the garden to the house, giving it a stronger sense of permanence. Color comes into play when each area is given its own palette of hues. Like rooms in your home, the garden settings can have different color themes. As you walk from one area to the next, the change in colors signals a clear transition. The blue border pictured here clearly defines this space, giving it its own character and style. The next area, through the pillared archway, will present a different combination of colors. Varying the color themes helps to make each area unique and memorable.

Establish One Color Theme Per Garden Room

After creating canvases in your garden, you are ready to apply your selection of colors to each garden setting. Just as you wouldn't paint every wall in your living room a different color, a garden room looks best when all the hues are coordinated into a color scheme. This creates a feeling of unity in the design and gives each space its own character and style.

Color is one of the most powerful tools you have for creating an atmosphere or mood. Inside our homes, we may be energized by a citrus-hued bathroom and lulled to sleep by a bedroom's powder blue walls. In that same way, choose colors for your garden settings that match the activity you have planned for each area. For instance, if you want to shelter a quiet spot for reading just outside your master bedroom, soothing colors in blues, purples, and whites help set a relaxing mood. On the other hand, if the same space was designed to be an outdoor entertainment area, a robust palette of yellow, red, and orange might be a better choice.

Some of the most dramatic and memorable gardens have been developed around a single color. In its purest form, this color scheme consists of the various tints and shades of one and only one color. (A tint is a lighter hue of the color, and a shade is darker.) An example would be a red garden with various tints of pink and a deep shade of red giving way to dark maroon. Visualize a summer annual flower border planted with the deep burgundy color of 'Love-Lies-Bleeding' next to maroon-colored coleus and a range of pink to magenta cosmos, and you can begin to see the possibilities of such a color scheme.

If you have a favorite color, there are different ways to develop the idea. Sections within a long mixed-color border can be expressed in a single color separated from the other color combinations with neutral-colored plants, such as gray foliage. Or if you like to change things up, you can alter single-color areas of your garden with the seasons. Whatever application you choose, the challenge with this approach is finding enough plants that can carry the color convincingly through the time period you choose.

Although these types of gardens are referred to by one color name, such as a blue garden, in reality there are no totally monochromatic gardens; various shades of flowers, foliage, and bark are always part of the combination. The famous White Garden created by Vita Sackville-West at Sissinghurst, England, has inspired countless gardeners, including myself, but even Vita referred to it as her "gray, green, and white garden."

Photographs of Sissinghurst in winter reveal the strong framework of structural plants essential to making monochromatic gardens work: tall green hedges and clipped box compartments contain the effusive plantings of white flowers and silver foliage. Green and gray foliage is also interspersed to separate the multitude of white shades, giving each one a distinct space in which to shine. There are even a few touches of pale pastels to soften the brilliance of the unrelieved white.

When I made my first white garden, I bought white plants with utter abandon. I tried anything—if it bloomed white or had white variegation or silvery gray foliage I had to have it. After the third season, I had my fill of all white and the garden began to transform into an "almost white" garden. I started slipping in other colors, first pale lavender, and then over time, I became bolder with purple and pinks. This monochromatic phase of my life taught me the importance of gray, texture, and forms, and that eventually led me to the appeal of other color families.

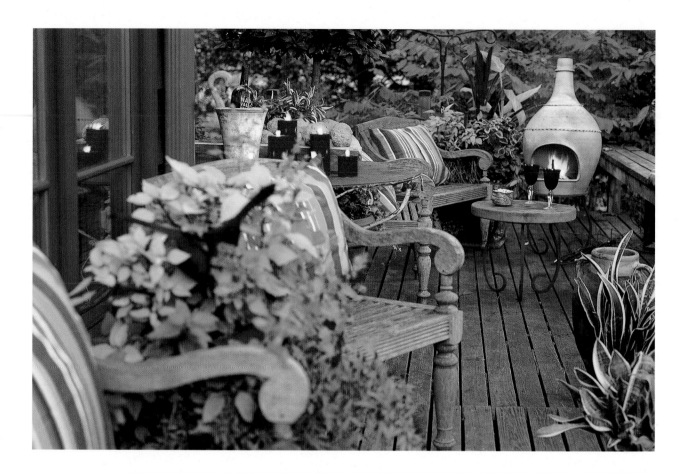

Above: Although multi-hued, this deck features a defined set of colors that infuses the setting with a well-coordinated color theme. The striped pillows offer an array of colors that are repeated in the garden room's accents. **Opposite, above left:** Like foot-candles, the light-colored pansies and stately white tulips, highlighted in silvery foliage, luminesce in the near dark. **Above right:** A quiet corner of my garden is awash in white flowers during the spring. To keep single-color gardens from becoming too one-dimensional, use a variety of bloom sizes and shapes as well as textured foliage at different heights. **Below left:** This cluster of containers offers a study in closely related cool colors. The blue cone-shaped flowers of the grape hyacinths are an easy-on-the-eye match for the purple irises in the nearby pot. Behind them, a container of violas is ready to join the blend. **Below right:** Mixing cool and neutral colors often results in a satisfying composition. Here a drift of purple torenias grows next to the just emerging blossoms of 'Autumn Joy' sedum.

If you find the single-color garden too restrictive, you may prefer to widen the palette to include a blend of colors from the same color family. The hues in these color schemes are closely related: for example, blue, blue-violet, and violet. When you add the tints and shades, this range of hues gives you more variety and is easier to work with than the single-color approach.

When these "cousin colors" from the same family of hues are in a garden setting, they have certain effects on the mood and spatial character of the setting. Warm colors, such as red, red-orange, orange, yellow-orange, peach, salmon, and yellow seem to come forward, giving an area the appearance of a smaller space. When used in a design scheme, they add the equivalent of warmth and sunshine. On the other hand, cool colors remind us of water and sky, so when we see them, they feel expansive.

In developing color schemes using related hues, the proportion of colors in the composition is based on your preferences.

Another option in developing a color scheme is to combine colors from different families. In its simplest form, this may involve choosing two colors, one from each family, such as blue from the cool side and white from the neutral side.

If you mix three or more contrasting colors, it is important to maintain a certain ratio for each color in the composition so the palette is balanced. Follow these general guidelines to keep your color selections in pleasing proportions. First, choose one dominant or key color from the group. This color will represent about 50 percent of your garden palette. Make sure it works well with any large existing color blocks in your garden, such as your house, the garage, any patio or deck flooring you may have, or even a fence.

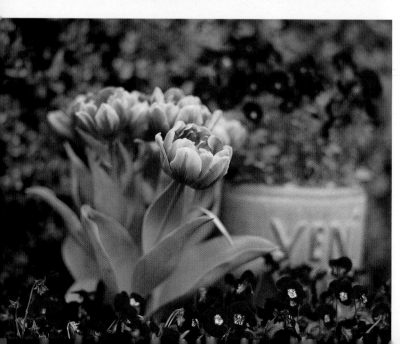

Next, consider what plants or objects you'll use to represent that color. As with the single color approach, be sure there are enough plants that grow well in your area to carry your leading color from spring through fall. Refer to the color directories in Part Three to assist you.

If pink is the dominant color, plants that might be listed include drifts of pink tulips in spring along with the pink blossoms of crabapple. By mid-spring, beauty bush, pink roses and showy primrose could help carry the theme forward. As summer begins, pink cosmos, phlox, and cleome would fill the border, followed by pink salvias and mums to finish the season in the fall.

The next step is to select three more colors to contrast or harmonize with your dominant color. Since the leading color will be about 50 percent of your garden's color scheme, pick a second color and think of it as filling about 25 percent of your garden's palette. The third color will play a smaller role at 15 percent, and the last color should be selected to bring in just a sparkle or accent to the other colors at 10 percent. The idea is to keep some equilibrium between the colors to maintain the integrity of the color theme. The colors you choose and their ratio to one another is what creates a sense of harmony in the design.

These recommended percentages are merely guidelines to help you become comfortable trying out various mixes of colors. The fun in working out these compositions is developing your own formula to create the most visually stimulating combinations. Play with the ratios until the results are pleasing.

Just like any good recipe, once you get all your main ingredients combined, it takes some extra seasoning to really bring out the best flavor in the dish. The same is true when mixing up a garden's color theme. In this case the seasoning to add to the mix is a sprinkling of a few neutral colors. As mentioned before, even though this color category is called neutral, it plays a very active role in enhancing color combinations. When blended into a garden's palette, neutrals either brighten, harmonize, or tone down the mix of colors. So as you create your color combinations, determine which quality you'd like to add and select the associated color.

Top left: Light and dark shades of the same color create a pleasing, easy-on-the-eye combination. **Center left:** All-white gardens are beautiful but require a good mix of contrasting textures, bloom shapes, and heights so the eye can appreciate each variety. **Left:** Contrasting hues from the warm- and cool-color families heighten the visual impact of each.

NEUTRAL COLOR	QUALITY
White and variegated white	Illuminates and adds sparkle.
Chartreuse and variegated yellow	Good with warm colors. Electrifies and excites.
Gray and glaucous green	Mixes beautifully with cool and pastel colors. Effective between contrasting colors. Calms and harmonizes.
Basic greens and browns	Dominant background color. Grounds and anchors. Blends with natural materials like wood, stone, and earth.
Black/burgundy	Sultry, moody. Creates visual depth and adds mystery.

Here are a few color combinations to spark your imagination:

DOMINANT COLOR	ADDITIONAL COLORS	NEUTRAL COLORS
Lavender	Purple, yellow, magenta	Gray or variegated
Red	Purple, violet, pink	Black
Magenta	Orange, purple, yellow	Chartreuse

Left: Various shades of purple pansies, nemesia, and clematis 'Anna Louise' are accented with yellow and magenta *Osteospermum* Cape Daisy and the chartreuse foliage of creeping Jenny.

Color Glossary

HUE: Another name for color.

VALUE: Relates to tint tone and shade, the lightness or darkness of a color.

DOMINANT COLOR: Key or leading color in a combination of colors, representing approximately 50 percent of the color theme.

SECOND COLOR: Color that harmonizes or contrasts with the dominant color, representing approximately 25 percent of the color theme.

THIRD COLOR: Color that is a neutral or from the same color family as the dominant or second color, representing 15 percent of color theme.

ACCENT COLOR: Hue selected to give the color scheme extra vitality, representing 10 percent of the total.

Right: Spring erupts in shades of pink and white. Azaleas and tulips are the early bloomers that define the color theme in this semi-shady part of my garden. **Opposite, above:** As the season progresses, early spring's cool color theme can be expressed in different plants. Here a range of pink impatiens, astilbe, and roses is combined with variegated hostas and ivy to extend the palette into early summer. **Opposite, below:** Before I spend time and money on a new color theme in the borders of my garden, I plant a version of the color combinations in various containers to see how they look. Once I get the ratio of hues just right, I feel more confident in making my plant selections for the larger landscape.

activity

Be a maverick and create a "paint sample" container by combining daring colors. Experiment and if you like what you see, expand the planting composition into the landscape. This will give you a chance to see how the colors work together before you invest in plants on a larger scale.

activity

Create an abundance of blooms by filling several large, frostproof containers with spring-flowering bulbs. The trick to this project is to pick bulbs that flower at the same time. For maximum impact, layer them in the container as if you were making lasagna. Pack in a layer of tall-growing bulbs (such as pink tulips) eight inches deep and "shoulder to shoulder" in the container. The bulbs can be touching each other but not the sides of the container. Cover with three inches of soil, and then add a layer of low-growing bulbs such as deep blue grape hyacinths. Cover them with another five inches of soil and an inch of mulch. Water the container well.

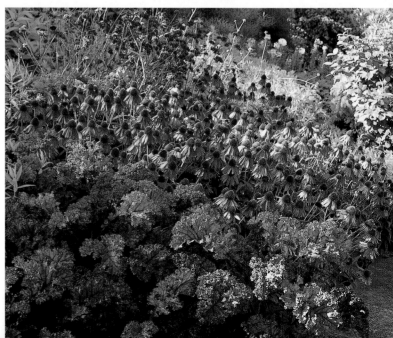

Make Bold Brush Strokes on Your Garden Canvas

"Now I really feel the landscape, I can be bold and include every tone of blue and pink: it's enchanting, it's delicious." — Claude Monet

Color *is* delicious! And, as Monet suggested, it should be used generously. As you develop the color themes for your garden rooms, be generous with your plantings and make strong statements with large expanses of color. It is best to be bold and simple rather than timid and jumbled.

Think of these broad sweeps of color within your landscape as if they were brush strokes upon a canvas. While the plants and objects within your garden add color, it is also their texture, size, shape, and structure that lend an expressive character to the setting. These additional qualities can be used in a garden's design in the same way that artists use them to add defining characteristics to their paintings. Think of the bold, impasto strokes of van Gogh's paintings, Monet's vigorous lines loaded with pure colors, or Seurat's pointillistic application of color. Similarly, the texture and shapes of plants and objects can develop a distinct emotional expression in your garden creations.

As a garden history student in England I toured many of the country's finest gardens and recorded my visits with hundreds of color photographs. On one occasion, I accidentally filled my camera with black-and-white film, and when it was developed, I was surprised to see the prints were not in color. I was about to toss them out, but at the last moment I decided to take a closer look. With the color drained from the pictures, I was able to see other components of the garden's design. The photos revealed how the plants' shapes and textures worked together to create an expressive quality in each garden scene. Studying those pictures awakened me to the underlying structure beneath the colors of the flowers and foliage. I realized it was the partnership of these elements, not just color alone, that made the gardens so magical.

As we "paint" with flowers and foliage, our compositions can be more satisfying if we use the texture and shapes of plants as the underlying configuration for our color schemes. While color undoubtedly helps us set the mood in the garden, this element alone is not enough to carry the composition. The emotional side of our personality responds to color, while our rational side seeks structure. Balance is achieved when the color scheme is combined with a pleasing mix of textures and forms in a way that keeps the eye and the imagination engaged.

To effectively weave these components together, it is important to understand how plants grow and change form over time. Look at the basic bloom and inflorescence shapes illustrated on the next page to help you begin to recognize how certain plants give your borders the feel of large and expressive brush strokes.

With consideration given to the various textural expressions that can be combined with the color schemes in your garden, follow nature's guide as you plant with abundance. Walk through a woodland or meadow and notice how the plants are growing in colonies and drifts. Groves of trees, clusters of wildflowers, and tangles of vines are all part of the profusion of plants found along the way. When we follow this lead in our gardens, the

Below: Studying black-and-white images, such as this one I took in England, helps me appreciate the "understudy" roles that texture, shape, and form play to support the color themes in a garden. **Opposite, above left:** Concentrated bursts of color in bold forms, such as this container of 'Menton' tulips, make a stronger impact than the same color in light, wispy plants. **Opposite, right:** Notice how the eye appreciates the variety of shapes and textures, particularly in settings with just a few colors. **Opposite, below left:** Placing two very different textures and forms side by side helps us appreciate the distinct qualities of each. The feathery plumes of purple fountain grass stand in stark contrast to the broad dark purple leaves of 'Black Knight' canna. **Opposite, below right:** Use plant forms to give expression to your palette. The purple coneflower blooms appear almost as colored dots in the landscape, while the crinkled leaves of ornamental kale are like short brush strokes of color.

Basic Plant Forms

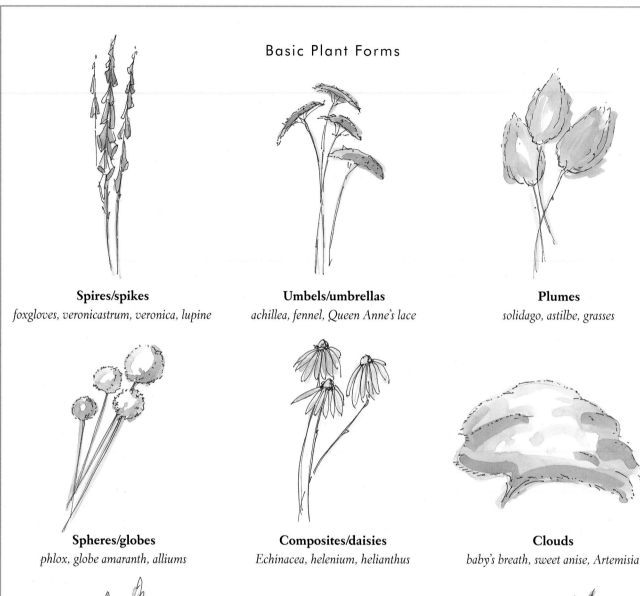

Spires/spikes

foxgloves, veronicastrum, veronica, lupine

Umbels/umbrellas

achillea, fennel, Queen Anne's lace

Plumes

solidago, astilbe, grasses

Spheres/globes

phlox, globe amaranth, alliums

Composites/daisies

Echinacea, helenium, helianthus

Clouds

baby's breath, sweet anise, Artemisia

Candelabra

turkscap lilies, yucca, galtonia

Trumpets

lilies, daylilies, brugmansia

Foxtails

fountain grass, millet, cattails, sanguisorba

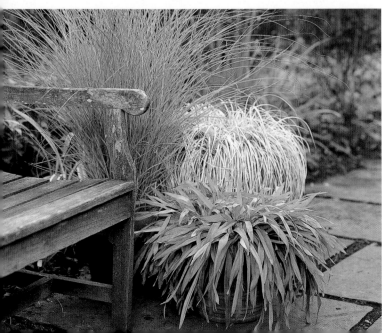

plantings appear spontaneous and comfortable. By assembling plants in groupings of three, five, or seven, the arrangement seems less contrived and artificial than those that are lined up rigidly along the edge of a bed or lawn.

There are several types of annuals, perennials, and bulbs that will help you create this abundant look with little effort. They are known as increasers, spreaders, or hardy volunteers. They are ideal when you want to add masses of color because they create lots of visual impact and come back each year without replanting.

Since the annuals are self-sowing, you can never be quite sure where they will pop up, and I love that spontaneous quality. I use them in areas of my garden where they can grow freely and fill in with other perennials. Some of the best hardy volunteers are larkspur, nicotiana, cleome, bachelor's buttons, and globe amaranth. They come in a range of colors, so use the variety that works best with your color scheme.

There are also several perennials that will colonize, clump, and spread. Some of my favorites are daylilies, irises, purple coneflower, sedums, hostas, bee balm (*Monarda*), and phlox. Bulbs that will naturalize to give you big drifts of color include daffodils, crocus, muscari, scillas, and leucojum. Again, each plant comes in a range of colors, so choose the cultivars that are right for your garden palette.

One note of caution: There are some prolific plants, such as mint, that can become garden thugs. They start out as well-behaved companions, but soon take hold and take over. If you have any doubts, check with nurseries and gardening friends so you can steer clear of these invasive plants.

Whether you are creating a garden from the ground up or have a mature landscape, you are better off identifying what I call "workhorse" plants to use as large blocks of color in your garden. These plants are easy-care, vigorous, and dependable varieties that are well suited for your area. Look around the neighborhood or in your own garden for the trees, shrubs, perennials, and annuals that are the most reliable under a variety of conditions.

Top: Spheres, stars, and spikes are found in the flower forms of 'New Dawn' climbing rose, 'Mrs. Cholmondeley' clematis, and tall blue larkspur. **Center:** Bright round balls of white zinnias appear to float in a cloud of smoky gray 'Powis Castle' artemisia while the 'Siskiyou Pink' butterfly blossoms fill the air. **Left:** A trio of grasses illustrates how colors work with the shape and form of the leaves to create a variety of expressions. In the foreground, the wide blue-green straplike foliage of 'Blue Bunny' carex contrasts with the nearly white weeping stands of 'Evergold' variegated carex and the sprays of 'Morning Light' miscanthus.

| FRAME THE VIEW |

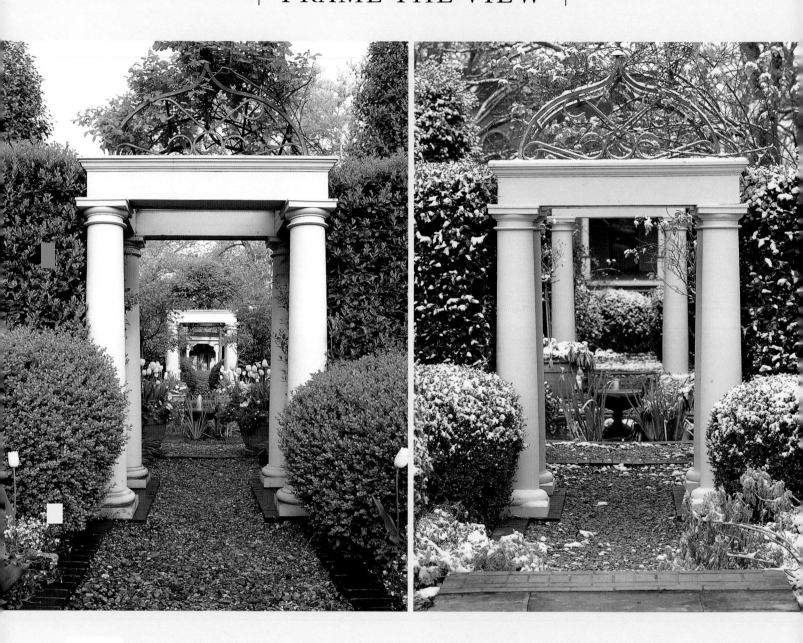

Framed views are powerful elements in garden design. This method is used to draw attention to an object or scene. When you gaze across your property, there are countless places to observe, everything from the neighbor's house to a container of flowers on the front step. By choosing which views you want to frame, you create the opportunity to develop a strong line of site from one point to the next while screening out distractions. Color helps to direct the focus of attention. The white arbors that frame the view into my fountain garden act as a neutral outline to the scene beyond. Much like a white mat that surrounds a work of art, they serve to direct the eye toward the object in the middle. Depending on the situation, the color of the frame can either serve as a neutral border or as part of the picture. Painted red, the arbors would become the focus of attention, rather than the element that holds the view.

Frame Your Work

The next important lesson in designing colorful garden rooms is to learn when and how to give color combinations a rest. Imagine a room that has several large paintings. The frames have been removed and the canvases are hung so the sides of the paintings touch one another, encircling the room. Without picture frames and some wall space between the paintings, you can't fully appreciate each work of art. The same is true in a garden that has no pauses between its compositions of color. To be able to see and experience each arrangement, it is important to separate the color groupings.

Legendary gardener Gertrude Jekyll understood this phenomenon and used it effectively in the broad canvas of her English garden at Munstead Woods. In the main flower border she used pale pastel colors at the outer ends of the border, intensifying the effect by using harmonious shades of warm golds and scarlets at the center. The movement through the color cycle was designed to alternately saturate and soothe the eye, much in the same way that a well-planned dinner alternately excites and soothes the taste buds.

She took this effect even further in creating multiple gardens, designing each one around a single color theme. In one area, the visitor would walk through hot-colored borders where Jekyll knew the eye would be filled and saturated with the strong red, orange, and yellow colors. She placed a yew arch just at the point where you would leave that area and enter into the next garden room. The next garden was filled with gray foliage and white, lilac, purple, and pink flowers. So after journeying through the hot-colored borders and standing in the arch, the visitor suddenly turned to see the gray garden. The strong contrast in colors was stunning, luminous, and refreshing and the pause between rooms made the effect even more powerful.

A transparent screen of plants through which you view other plants in a border also creates a veil of separation between colors. These "see-through plants" create a soft haze that alters

Above: Three large terra-cotta pots of lavender give this long flower border a pause. In the background, an open-roofed arbor also serves as a break between garden rooms. **Right:** A long wall helps to manage an elevation change in the lawn and a color line between the plants. On one side, compact white shrub roses hug the wall, while on the other side, pink spiraea and spires of blue catmint bloom.

Left: Giving the open sky a framework of flowered branches is another way to modify the feel of an outdoor area. **Below:** Like a gauzy veil, the plumes of the ornamental grass 'Karl Forester' soften the color of the bright yellow coneflowers and the scene beyond. **Opposite:** Several rose-covered arches at Old Westbury Garden create a tunnel of color as a transition between the rose garden and the next area of the landscape.

the color of a composition, influencing the mood of a garden space. I like to use these delicate curtains or natural scrims toward the front of a planted bed and then plant bold textured foliage or blooms in the back as a focal point.

The idea of arranging tall plants at the front of a border and potentially obscuring the view of other plants behind it may feel counterintuitive. But instead of following the traditional tall-to-short arrangement of plants, envision clouds of pink summer phlox 'Bright Eyes' viewed through the lanky stems and lavender colored blooms of *Verbena bonariensis.* Or imagine a bold drift of salmon-colored daylilies through the misty haze of bronze fennel or the delicate blades of an ornamental grass. I liken this to a light wash an artist might apply to a painting to create an atmospheric touch.

I think it is better to use this technique sparingly yet deliberately when certain combinations of color are desired and to give a border some visual variety.

Breaks also help you to separate two clashing colors in the landscape. Incompatible hues in a flower border or the

activity

Squint your eyes and look at an area of garden with a blurred, almost impressionistic view of what is there. This will help you see what works and where you need a pause to separate incompatible areas. Consider the devices you could use to create these resting places for the eye.

See-Through Plants

Stipa gigantea (giant feather grass)
Sanguisorba officinalis (great burnet)
Thalictrum polygamum (meadow rue)
Thalictrum aquilegifolium (columbine meadow rue)
Foeniculum vulgare 'Rubrum' (bronze fennel)
Molinia caerulea (moor grass)
Verbena bonariensis (verbena-on-a-stick)
Gaura
Sanguisorba tenuifolia 'Alba' (Japanese burnet)
Miscanthus sinensis (silver grass)
Muhlenbergia capillaris (muhly grass)
Patrinia

clashing color of a neighbor's house can be reasons to create a break or pause in the land-scape. A simple divider such as a green hedge, neutral-colored foliage, an arbor, trellis, or other types of screens are just a few of the options you can employ to prevent a jarring encounter.

The lawn, sky, water, sidewalk, and driveway are also elements in the landscape that can either create a devised pause, or, in some cases, be the part of a garden's design that needs to be softened. For instance, a sidewalk leading up to your house can offer a break between two color compositions on either side. But a large driveway may overpower the landscape and need to be softened with plantings of shrubs to break up its visual impact. Scaling back the lawn to wide strips of grass between the flower beds keeps it in balance with other garden elements so it gives the eye a rest, just as hedges, arches, and low walls can do.

In painting, the use of the same colors in various parts of a composition draws the eye from one area to the next. Strong splashes of color that appear at regular intervals keep the eye and mind visually stimulated. In that same way, repeating blocks of color rhythmically through a border allows the viewer to appreciate a composition of color and then see it re-peated again.

To create this effect, divide the length of the bed into five-foot intervals and then fill a section of the border with a color combination of six or so plants assembled in a pleasing arrangement. Before repeating the color combination again, create a pause in the border by planting a cluster of transitional plants in a harmonizing color such as a gray or green, and then add your next color grouping. Continue this pattern down the length of the bed. In this situation the pauses or breaks between the groupings create enough definition to set up an interesting rhythm of color.

Below: Bright red tulips create a polka-dot effect as they emerge from a bed of 'Powis Castle' artemesia. This neutral gray background serves to hold the pattern of colors together. **Below right:** This long herbaceous border repeats distinct blocks of color that are separated by neutral-color plantings to keep the eye moving along the bed.

TEXTURE, PATTERN, AND RHYTHM

Texture, pattern, and rhythm can be thought of as partners for colors in a garden design. For example, imagine all the plants pictured here in green. With uniform colors, the interest in the design would be created by the different textures of the leaves and flowers, the pattern in the tulip's striped petals and the rhythmic nature of the steps and clusters of tulips along the walkway. By recognizing these elements and using them in conjunction with color, your garden will have more depth and character. Just as combining two contrasting colors (such as blue and yellow) sets off both hues, placing fuzzy leaves next to glossy foliage further heightens the visual appeal. Adding patterns of variegated foliage or repeating motifs such as an X in a door, gate, and trellis helps to create a continuum or pattern within a garden's design. The placement of objects, such as containers or groupings of plants at rhythmic intervals, also sets up a visual beat in a garden. Color acts to either heighten or blend these elements into the fabric of the garden.

Explore the Effects of Light and Time

"Should it not be remembered that in setting a garden we are painting—a picture of hundreds of feet or yards instead of so many inches, painted with living flowers and seen by open daylight—so that to paint it rightly is a debt that we owe to the beauty of flowers and to the light of the sun." —William Robinson, The English Flower Garden and Home Grounds, *1883*

While many correlations can be drawn between designing a color scheme for an interior room and an outdoor garden setting, the effect that light has on color in an outdoor setting is one aspect that differs. Inside our homes, no matter if it's day or night, the colors in the rooms appear the same with the constancy of interior lighting. But outside, natural light creates dramatic color changes throughout the day.

Artist Claude Monet created several landscape paintings from the same perspective during different times of the day, like the famous series of haystack paintings that he worked on over a period of two years. Monet painted the haystacks in sunny and gray weather, in the fog and with glazes of snow. Working directly from nature, he captured the dramatic effect light has on color, illustrating how the same fixed subject displays a completely different palette of colors in the ever-changing light.

You can experience this phenomenon for yourself by observing an area of your garden as the sun rises, and again at high noon. Bathed in the warm glow of early-morning light, colors appear rich and saturated, but by midday, under the glare of a bright sun, those same colors may look washed out. In the golden light of morning, red flowers appear more orange, while in the bluer light of early evening, the red deepens and becomes almost purple.

Keeping this in mind can help you enhance your color experience. For instance, at the end of the day you may enjoy relaxing on your east-facing front porch. You may love dark and deeply saturated colors, but as the sun sets in the west and the light dims on the porch, these colors may lose their luster. Adding pastel, white, or silvery plants into the mix will brighten the compositions so they can be enjoyed into the evening as well.

If you have a shady area that you'd like to brighten, illuminate it with a swath of light-colored plants, such as white and pale pink impatiens. Then add some foliage plants with bold, white variegated leaves, such as hosta, caladium, or variegated Solomon's seal. These luminous colors reflect light and will sparkle in the shade. To blend this patch of brightness into areas of the garden with less shade, mix in plants with less variegation and then gradually intermingle them with green foliage plants. Bright colors in shade that transition into variegated plants and finally to green allow the pool of color to lighten dark areas of the garden and then fade naturally into the landscape.

Conversely, dark-colored plants can create areas of depth and dimension in bright areas. Pockets of deeply saturated flowers and foliage help to break up the sameness in borders filled with light-colored plants. The deeper colors appear to recede, adding visual dimension to the bed.

Weaving the threads of your garden's color theme into the tapestry of the landscape's seasonal hues is another way to work with light and time. While annuals often stay colorful through the growing season, most perennials come on and off the stage according to

Above: The soft glow of candlelight held in small glass jars and suspended from the branches of a tree adds warm spots of color as the sun sets. **Opposite, above left:** Encased in frozen rain from a wintry storm, my garden has been transformed into an ice palace. Seasonal changes often create an extreme color makeover in the garden. The fun is in finding ways to use Mother Nature's ever-changing palette to your advantage. **Opposite, above right:** Soft lights create a welcoming glow in the pool house. **Opposite, below left:** Positioning outdoor rooms to capture the last rays of daylight encourages family and friends to gather and enjoy the setting. Reflective wall surfaces, large arched openings, and the wall-mounted sconces enhance the mood. **Opposite, below right:** Painted surfaces in the garden change as the sun moves through the sky. This black iron chair takes on a blue cast at the end of the day. When applying indoor colors to an outdoor setting, I have found that it is best to lessen the intensity of the hue with a thin wash of gray. The indoor color seems to fit more comfortably in natural light when it is slightly toned down.

activity

Play up the light in your garden by positioning light-catching plants in strategic areas where they can catch the morning or evening rays of sun. Tall, delicate plants, such as salvia and verbena bonariensis, or grasses such as miscanthus, panicum, and stipa, are all good light catchers, beautiful when backlit by low-angle rays of light. Notice where the sun rises and sets on your garden so you can find the best place to display these plants. The seed heads of grasses also hold little beads of water that capture rays of light, creating a magical effect.

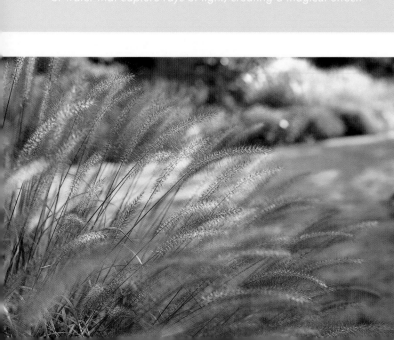

the time they bloom. A colorful plant enjoying a starring role during the spring may play second fiddle in nature's second act, summer. You can use this to your advantage to gently alter your color palette through the year. The key to making this approach work is to keep a constant color theme running through the garden as one color segues into the next. By choreographing your plants' bloom times when the brightenss of the leading color fades, it will be replaced with one of the supporting hues.

One way to understand this seasonal blooming choreography is to create bouquets of flowers at various times of the year to experiment with their color relationships. Also, keeping a journal that monitors when certain flowers begin to bloom and when they reach their peak is a good way to determine what can work in your garden before you purchase the first plant or sow any seeds. Record the mature height of the plants and any other observations, such as cultural notes and combinations.

Along with creating color palettes that blend with the seasons, consider adding objects that capture and display the elemental forces of nature, wind, water, and fire. The dynamic qualities of these life forces create a heightened sense of mystery and drama not available in interior rooms. Pools of water becomes liquid mirrors, reflecting the ever-changing hues of the sky as well as the colors in the landscape. Plants bob and weave in the wind, changing form and color as they bend and dip, revealing their hidden undersides. And who hasn't felt the primal pull to gather around an outdoor fire, transfixed by the golden flames as they dance in the dark?

Garden centers are full of products that can help you add these elements to your garden. Water gardens with beautiful aquatic plants, wall-mounted fountains, wind chimes, whirly-gigs, plants that move gracefully in the wind, chimineas, fire pits, and outdoor fireplaces are just a few of the features you can add to capture and display these natural elements, creating a more intriguing color scheme in your garden.

There are also many types of outdoor lighting that will enhance your gardens and entice you to enjoy your outdoor setting well into the night. Everything from path lights to tiki torches help to illuminate garden rooms, extending the enjoyment of your outdoor living spaces into the evening hours. When placing lighting in the garden, however, less is more.

Above left: A wall of mounted candles along the side of the house turns this area of the garden into a magical retreat. The pool of water draws in the last rays of light from the sky, creating a shimmering reflection.
Left: Feathered plumes of fountain grass transform into soft arcs of light in the late-afternoon sun.

| TIME AND MYSTERY |

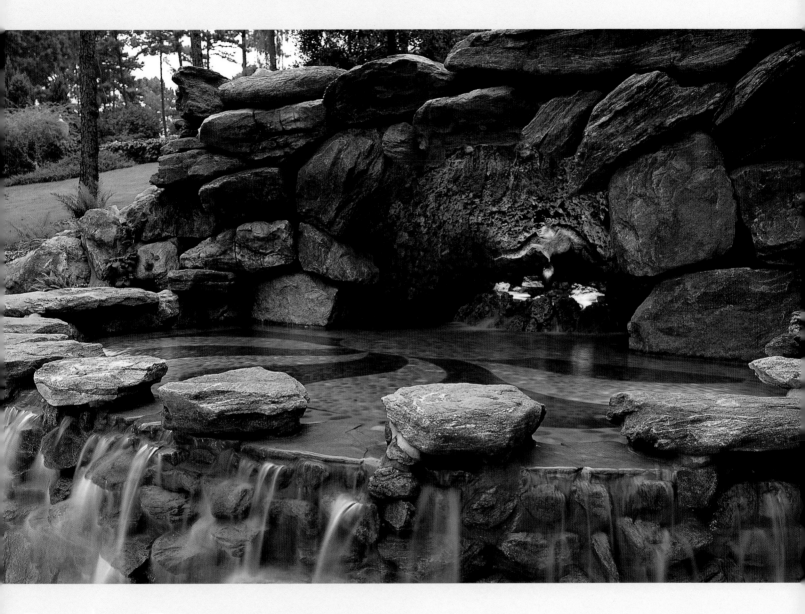

Weave elements of the unknown, the unseen, and the mysterious through your garden to make it a place of endless fascination. Who hasn't been enticed to walk a little farther by a glimpse of something interesting at the bend in a path? Creating a sense of anticipation and then rewarding the explorer for the effort are qualities worth developing in a garden. In the grotto pictured here, the glow of light under the moving water reflects on the time-worn rocks. Visitors are compelled to come closer to see what or who is crouching in the cave. Color adds to the drama with spots of bright light, earthy hues in the stone, and flowing blue water. Established gardens offer a sense of timelessness that is hard to duplicate in freshly planted areas. Consider using various painting techniques to help you instantly age objects such as containers, benches, and tables to give them a weathered patina.

Part Three

COLOR
EXPRESSIONS

COLOR EXPRESSIONS

ALL THROUGH OUR LIVES, ON BOTH A CONSCIOUS AND INTUITIVE LEVEL, WE MAKE CONNECTIONS BETWEEN colors in the landscape and the emotions they evoke. Consider the colors these classic tranquil images bring to mind: a soft pine needle path threading its way through a rich, verdant forest or a cool mountain stream bubbling over ancient water-worn boulders. By drawing on your own color associations, you can create a garden oasis that blends your personal tastes with the colors of your home.

> "*Color is mysterious, eluding definition; it is a subjective experience, a cerebral sensation depending on three related and essential factors: light, an object, and an observer.*"
> —ENID VERITY

To help you consolidate the rainbow of hues, this part of the book has been organized into three color groups referred to in Parts One and Two: cool, warm, and neutral. Each color group has an overview to give you an idea of how that color family can be used to its best effect. The members within each are then discussed in detail to offer you specific information about that color and to recommend seasonal plant combinations to try. The plants in this section are dependable examples that I have used in my garden designs. In the glossy section, you will find lists of specific varieties of shrubs, trees, vines, roses, and bulbs. The tables in the uncoated pages include perennials and annuals for each color. Together they will provide you with a "paint box" full of colorful choices. I hope this section will inspire you to explore the rich possibilities of creating color portraits in your garden home.

COOL
COLOR EXPRESSIONS

BLUE, LAVENDER TO PURPLE, PINK, MAGENTA

I must confess that when choosing colors for garden designs, I am inclined toward cool colors. These refreshing hues wear well through hot summer days. They mix easily together, creating all kinds of delicious combinations from the tones and shades of this family.

One factor to consider when developing a cool color scheme is to decide if you want that palette to dominate all year long. You may prefer to follow a more seasonal rotation in your garden. Some of the more compelling color schemes are those that incorporate this progressive transformation. However, if you have a small garden, it might be wise to stay with the cooler shades. As has been stated before, light colors in general and those that move to the bluest of hues alter our perception of space in a way that makes small areas feel more expansive. In diminutive patio gardens or outdoor places that could use a little more elbow room, these colors can help create the illusion of additional space.

Even if you choose a cool color palette, you aren't limited to draw all your colors from that side of the family. By mixing in a few warm colors you can brighten the composition. That's one of the reasons I like to mix blue and yellow together. This is especially true in areas of reduced light, where blue might become lost, so a pale yellow makes a good companion. Your eye is drawn first to the yellow hues, and then you notice the blue. The addition of a complementary color makes the composition more enlivening and a bit more intriguing.

To further explore how each cool color in the family can be articulated in your garden, this section is divided into four main colors: blue, lavender/purple, pink, and magenta, so you can consider each one individually.

Blue

In the garden, blue is the most coveted of colors, perhaps because there are so few flowers that are true blue. Many English gardeners consider the Blue Himalayan poppy to be the "gold standard" for the color. The flower is such an intense shade of blue that it almost looks artificial. I've never tried it because I've been told that it is very finicky and difficult to grow. Why struggle with something that is fussy when there are so many other good plant choices that can deliver equally satisfying results? I find it more gratifying to put my energy into growing more reliable plants and then experimenting with other combinations in new and exciting ways.

To create the best impact with blue flowers, try clustering them in several clumps to establish a pattern and rhythm within the border, such as patches of delphiniums planted at regular intervals along a fence. A band of blue pansies planted in a long sinuous line also makes a beautiful highlight along a path.

Some of the best blues in the garden come from bulbs, such as blue scilla naturalized among trees. One of my favorite combinations is blue violas with yellow miniature daffodils such as 'Hawera' and early pale pink tulips.

Opposite: This extreme close-up of the individual flowers that make up the ball-shaped bloom of Queen of the Nile (*Agapanthus*) helps to show off its vivid blue color.

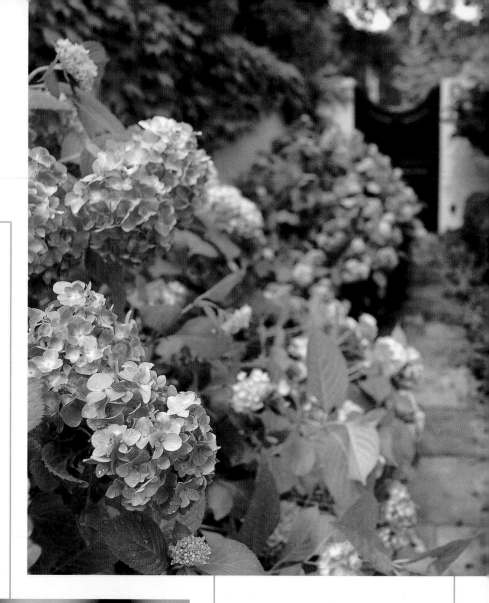

Blue Bulbs

Grape hyacinths: *Muscari armeniacum* 'Saffier', 'Cantab'; *M. aucheri* 'Blue Magic'; *M.* 'Valerie Finnis'
Hyacinths: *Hyacinthus* 'Delft Blue'
Spanish bluebells: *Hyacinthoides hispanica* 'Excelsior'
English bluebells: *Hyacinthoides non-scripta*
Quamash: *Camassia quamash* 'Blue Melody'
Dutch iris: 'Sky Beauty'
Reticulated iris: *Iris reticulata* 'Cantab'
Wood squill: *Scilla siberica* 'Spring Beauty'
Glory of the snow: *Chionodoxa forbesii*
Spring starflower: *Ipheion* 'Wisley Blue'
Striped Squill: *Puschkinia libanotica*

Blue Flowering Shrubs

Hydrangea: *Hydrangea macrophylla* 'Blue Wave', 'Nikko Blue'
Butterfly bush: *Buddleia davidii* 'Nanho Blue', 'Ellen's Blue'
California lilac: *Ceanothus delilianus* 'Gloire de Versailles', *C.* 'Victoria'
Bluebeard: *Caryopteris* x *clandonensis* 'Heavenly Blue'
Lilac: *Syringa vulgaris* 'Blue Skies', 'Little Boy Blue'
Viper's bugloss: *Echium vulgare*
Rose of sharon: *Hibiscus syriacus* 'Bluebird', 'Blue Satin'
Rosemary: *Rosmarinus officinalis* 'Tuscan Blue', 'Sawyer's Blue'

Blue Plant Combinations

SPRING *(shade)*	SUMMER *(sun)*	FALL *(sun)*
'Origami Blue and White' columbine	'Imperial Blue' plumbago	Hardy ageratum
Variegated Solomon's seal	'Lola' lantana	'Fireworks' goldenrod
'Camelot White' foxglove	'Morning Light' maiden grass	'Purple Dome' aster

Another stunning way to bring blue color into the garden is to plant hydrangeas such as the old-fashioned 'Nikko Blue' or 'Blue Wave' in a mass along the foundation of a house. For a lighter touch I've also used a lace cap hydrangea 'Serrata Blue Billow' to good effect. The bluish-lavender buddleia 'Nanho Blue' also makes a beautiful anchor at the back of the border.

An affliction that seems to be shared among many gardeners is the desire to introduce plants from "no grow" zones. These are specimens that are so outstanding that once you see them you immediately want them, but due to your garden's growing conditions, they couldn't survive. These cravings come upon me whenever I visit California and see their gorgeous California lilacs in bloom. What I wouldn't give to be able to have just one *Ceanothus delilianus* 'Gloire de Versailles' with its sky-blue flowers in my garden! When I share my enthusiasm about these plants, most Californians seem rather cavalier. Because they can grow them so easily in their area, the lilacs aren't considered special.

I also used to lust after the vivid blue ball-shaped flower clusters of agapanthus until I discovered that I could grow my own 'Lily of the Nile' in pots and then overwinter them in my potting shed. But I'm still scratching my head over how to grow a ceanothus; the shrub loves California's chalky alkaline soil and wouldn't survive in my clay soil. While I do very well with blue-eyed grass, somehow that offers little consolation.

Don't forget opportunities to add touches of blue to vertical surfaces in your garden. One of the great blue mixers in the plant world is clematis. It is a most social plant, climbing up walls, fences, buildings, and even other plants. There are so many beautiful blue varieties to choose from. I grow clematis 'Mrs. Cholmondeley' and delight in the way it scampers up my arbor. When its dessert-plate-size blooms open, it is a sight to behold.

If you are stymied by the task of locating enough blue plants to grow in your garden, don't forget blue accessories such as containers. The saturated color found in many glazed pots adds instant interest and is an easy way to extend your color theme.

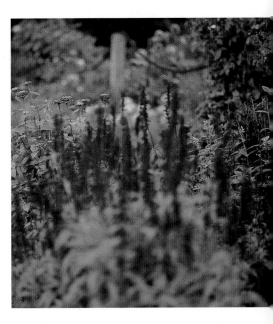

Above: Salvias are invaluable for providing the saturated blue color that gardeners crave. The mealycup sage (*Salvia farinacea* 'Victoria Blue') is only hardy to Zone 7 but is a fast grower that can be raised as an annual. **Opposite, above:** A line of 'Nikko Blue' hydrangeas creates a memorable walk down the pathway to the garden gate. **Opposite, below:** Graceful blue-petaled blossoms of this giant blue flag Louisiana iris (*Iris giganti-caerulea*) are held aloft on tall (nearly 4 foot) stems.

Opposite, above left: **Opposite, above left:** You'd be hard-pressed to find purple flowers more exotically beautiful than those of a passion vine. *Passiflora* 'Amethyst' ('Lavender Lady') puts on a profuse show of 4-inch flowers with deep violet crowns. **Above right:** This wisteria vine has grown into a tree-like form. The twining, woody plant becomes quite large and is generally long-lived. Unforgettably spectacular when in bloom, the plant's pendulous flowers shower the area in a sea of lavender. **Below left:** A close look at the flower clusters of 'Ayesha' hydrangea reveals the subtle color variations within its purple blooms. **Below right:** Striking yet simple, this purple and lavender border makes a big show with just a few varieties of purple plants. Abundance is the key to making a strong visual impact.

Lavender to Purple

The light side of this hue is lavender, a color often associated with a spring palette. One of the outstanding plants that represents this seasonal color is the wisteria vine. A stunning bloomer, this vigorous climber always evokes a strong response when it explodes into pendulous clusters of extremely fragrant lavender flowers. The vine is an effective way to elevate this color, giving the garden a lift. However, be warned that wisteria vines have the reputation as being the sumo wrestlers of the garden world. Once established, they require vigilant monitoring and aggressive pruning. Otherwise they can pull down trees and smother buildings with their heavy branch-like vines and long tentacles. Teach wisteria vines and other undisciplined plants some manners by growing them in containers. I've trained a pair of wisteria into well-behaved potted accents in front of my tool shed, where they wave a polite hello.

A less aggressive lavender/purple vine that still exhibits impressive coverage without the attitude is the morning glory. In the first years of my garden I had little in the way of height because most of the plants were small annuals and perennials. To bring an immediate sense of scale to the flower borders, I built some tuteurs, placed them in the beds, and planted morning glories around them. In just a few weeks the vines scaled the supports and opened their saucer-shaped blooms. They proved to be handsome backdrops for a foreground of cosmos, gomphrena, and celosia as well as other old-fashioned annuals.

Purple occupies the deeper range of this color. In its darker form purple takes on a more sultry and sexy quality. When placed in a border of lighter-colored plants, it adds visual weight and dimension to the color scheme. If you have a very linear bed with little depth, darker colors such as purple create a feeling of undulation as light-colored plants pop forward and the deep colors recede. The drama of plants with purple foliage and flowers is also effective in the back of the border and as a contrasting backdrop for lighter colors in the front of the bed. There are several plants with deep purple to burgundy foliage such as cordyline, canna, and coleus that are particularly effective when mixed with flowering plants in containers. The eye appreciates the contrast of the richly saturated foliage against the bloom of the flowers grown side by side.

One common mistake is to use purple hued plants too close together. I stumbled over that problem when I used a purple leafed barberry as a backdrop for a large planting of deep purple 'Caesars Brother' iris. Although appealing when viewed up close, from a distance the iris was lost because both colors were so deeply saturated and intense that the blooms of the iris disappeared against the foliage of the barberry. A softer lavender- or violet-colored iris would have been a better choice.

The challenge with using purple and other dark colors is that if you use them to excess, the garden becomes quite somber. I usually try to hold the line at not using more than 20 percent in a border. That's an approximation, but the idea is to stand back and evaluate the composition and to decide when enough is enough. A little goes a long way.

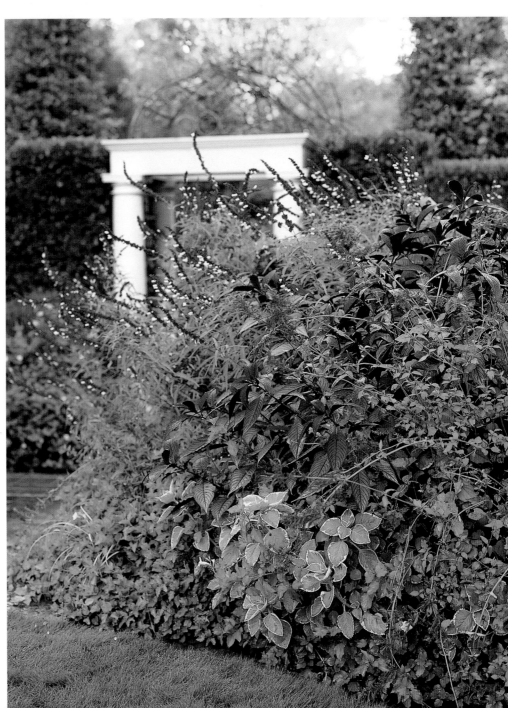

Purple or Lavender Vines

Clematis: *Clematis* 'Jackman's Superb', 'The President', 'Etoile Violette', 'Gipsy Queen', 'Blue Angel'
Japanese wisteria: *Wisteria floribunda* 'Royal Purple'
Cup and saucer vine: *Cobaea scandens*
Morning glory: *Ipomoea tricolor* 'President Tyler'
Sweet pea: *Lathyrus* 'Cupani Original'
Passionflower: *Passiflora caerulea*

Purple or Lavender Shrubs

Chaste tree: *Vitex agnus-castus*
Crape myrtle: *Lagerstroemia* 'Lipan', 'Zuni', 'Muskogee'
Lilac: *Syringa* 'Lilac Sunday', 'Lavender Lady', 'Excel'
Rhododendron: *Rhododendron* 'Blue Peter', 'Daphnoides', 'Blue Baron'
Butterfly bush: *Buddleia davidii* 'Black Knight', 'Lochinch'
Rose of sharon: *Hibiscus syriacus* 'Lavender Chiffon'
Hydrangea: *Hydrangea macrophylla*
Golden dewdrop: *Duranta erecta*
California lilac: *Ceanothus*
Potato bush: *Solanum crispum* 'Glasnevin'
Leptodermis: *Leptodermis oblonga*

Lavender/Purple Combinations

SPRING *(sun)*
'Silverlode' heuchera
'Penny White' and 'Penny Azure Twilight' violas
'Maureen' white tulip

SUMMER *(sun)*
'Indigo Spires' salvia
'Bright Eyes' phlox
Bronze fennel

FALL *(sun)*
Aster oblongifolius 'Raydon's Favorite'
'Golden Lace' patrinia
'Zebrinus' maiden grass

Pink

Pink is an agreeable color that is easy to work with in the garden. Whether it is a clear, soft angel-skin pink or something bordering on salmon, the range of pink colors is compatible with lots of other hues. Pink plants look more natural and carefree when planted in varying shades, from the hottest to the palest pinks rather than in all the same hue.

Since pink combines beautifully with so many other colors, it makes a beautiful backdrop in the border. Due to my weakness for old-fashioned roses and other pink flowering shrubs, I use them as anchors in my mixed borders. Pink is a natural leading color against a brown house. Just as baby blue and brown is a classic color combination, so is pink and brown.

Above: An impressive display of soft pink petunias bubbles out of a gray stone urn. When set in front of the slightly darker hued pink 'New Dawn' roses and the upright lavender flower spikes of 'Purple Smoke' baptisia, this cool color combination radiates quiet elegance.

Pink Flowering Shrubs

Weigela: *Weigela florida* 'Polka'

Beautybush: *Kolkwitzia amabilis* 'Pink Cloud'

Butterfly bush: *Buddleia davidii* 'Pink Delight'

Camellia: *Camellia japonica* 'Debutante', *C. sasanqua* 'Cleopatra', 'Winter's Star', 'Winter's Dream'

Flowering quince: *Chaenomeles japonica* 'Pink Lady', 'Toya Nishiki'

Crape myrtle: *Lagerstroemia* 'Osage', 'Choctaw', 'Caddo'

Oleander: *Nerium oleander* 'Mrs. Roeding', 'Shell Pink', 'Hardy Pink'

Rhododendron: *Rhododendron mucronulatum* 'Cornell Pink', *R. yakusimanum* 'Yaku Princess', 'Annie H. Hall'

Summersweet: *Clethra alnifolia* 'Ruby Spice'

Hydrangea: *Hydrangea macrophylla* 'Ayesha', 'Pia', 'Forever Pink'

Azalea: *Azalea* 'George Tabor', 'Pink Pearl'

Dwarf spirea: *Spirea japonica* 'Little Princess'

Indian hawthorne: *Raphiolepsis umbellata* 'Eleanor Taber', 'Pink Lady'

Rose escallonia: *Escallonia exoniensis* 'Frades', *E. langleyensis* 'Apple Blossom'

Lilac: *Syringa villosa* 'Miss Canada'

A fun and daring color combination is mixing pink with orange. Not long ago, I would have considered this to be an ill-matched twosome, but then I saw a flower arrangement that changed my mind. It hosted a wide range of pinks and, surprisingly, lots of orange. Although the hot-color family holds less appeal to me for color schemes in the garden, once I saw orange combined with pink I began to consider using these colors in new ways. Now, for the qualifier: while I am willing to add orange with pink, I have found that a pink and yellow composition doesn't excite me. The colors seem to be disagreeable companions unless the yellow is the palest, buttery yellow.

I'm not alone in having strong preferences for certain color combinations. When recently mentioning to a friend a hot-colored flower border that we had seen together, she suddenly said, "Oh, do you mean the retina-irritant border?" Her garden color preferences leaned more toward the cool-color range of blues, lavenders, and particularly soft pinks. Instead of drawing on hot colors to add spark to her border, she used smatterings of chartreuse as an electrifying accent. Upon seeing the results, I concluded that when pink is combined with gray it takes on an air of respectability, but when chartreuse is tossed into the mix, it turns into something quite sassy.

Another way to brighten pink is with the addition of white. Try mixing them using the same plant varieties, such as pink and white dianthus, pink and white nicotiana, or pink and white Asiatic lilies. Various shades of pink combined with white variegated plants help to illuminate shady areas. My favorite way to add pink and white to my garden is with roses. No other flower encompasses all the shades of pink better than the rose.

Above: A long row of French hydrangea with purple centers and pink lace-capped inflorescence makes a striking background border. The flowers on most hydrangeas are pH-sensitive, so by adjusting the soil chemistry, you can create various colors: dark purple or blue flowers in acidic soil, white or dull green in neutral earth, and pink in alkaline soil. **Opposite, left:** I rely on the tall, stately form of Louisiana iris in my garden designs. The plants thrive in well-watered, rich garden soil as well as at pond margins, so they are ideal around water features. The tall strap-like foliage gives the garden a vertical lift, and the graceful, flattish blossoms flower above and among the leaves. **Opposite, above right:** While heritage varieties of roses are my weakness, I couldn't pass up the modern cultivar 'Eden' (also known as 'Pierre de Ronsard'); this vigorous pink climber has plenty of old-fashioned charm. **Opposite, below right:** A fountain of pink blooms shoots like a geyser from the corner of this house. This weeping form of a flowering cherry tree creates a dramatic focal point in spring.

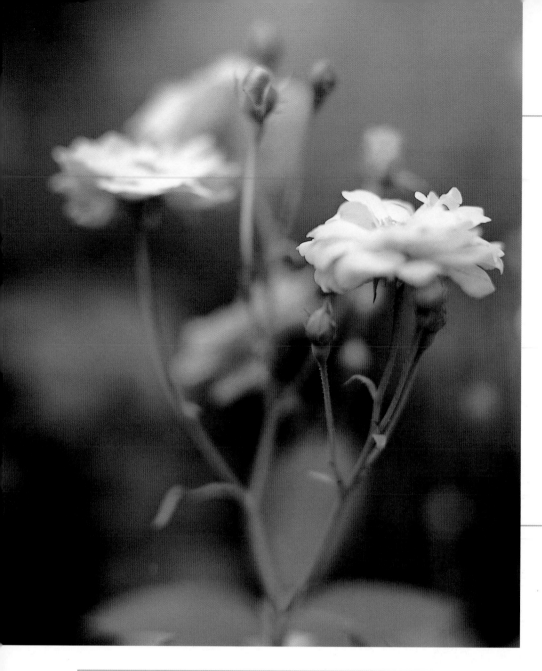

Pink Shrubs and Climbing Roses

'Climbing Pinkie'

'Pinkie'

'Caldwell Pink'

'Climbing Cécile Brünner'

'Zephirine Drouhin'

'New Dawn'

'Jeanne La Joie' (miniature climber)

'Clair Martin'

'Blushing Knockout'

'Sarah Van Fleet'

'Marie Pavie'

'Bonica'

'Carefree Delight'

'China Doll'

'The Fairy'

'Lovely Fairy'

Pink Plant Combinations

SPRING (*sun*)

'Carefree Wonder' rose

'Trailing Plum' coleus

'Tapien Pink' verbena

SUMMER (*sun*)

'Sonata Pink' cosmos

'David' phlox

'Powis Castle' artemisia

FALL (*sun*)

'Clara Curtis' chrysanthemum

'Togen' toadlily

'Evergold' variegated sedge

Magenta

This clear blue-red color is a fantastic mixer with all the other members of the cool family. While it may be too intense to serve as the leading color, it is perfect as an accent or an anchoring hue.

I rely on the magenta blooms of the old-fashioned shrub rose 'Russell's Cottage' as a seasonal color foundation in my front border. The plant has grown so vigorously that it stretches up into a neighboring elm tree. In spring, the shrub turns into a geyser of magenta blooms, spraying the tree with color. This fount of violet-purple roses makes it a "stop the car" plant. And if that wasn't enough, when warm breezes blow through the garden, the sweet perfume of these heavenly blossoms is carried right into the house. While it only flowers once, it is such a singular moment that I look forward to it with great anticipation. As the blossoms fade, the shrub quietly settles into the background and its glossy green foliage becomes a dark canvas for other flowering plants. Its role in the garden changes with the seasons. In spring, the rose is a majestic focal point and a color anchor. Through summer and fall, it turns into a neutral canvas for other colors, and in the winter, its branches still serve to outline the framework of the garden room.

There are several other magnificent roses with different bloom cycles that can help you capture the range of this richly satisfying color. Depending on the plant, the blooms can border on pink embracing blue, or take on the look of crushed raspberries. In its more intense hue, it can appear violet.

The rose that pushes magenta to the extreme is 'Veilchenblau', which dances on the purple side of violet. Like other shades within this range, it is so intense that it is best used as an anchor in a composition of other cool colors. However, if you are feeling adventurous and want to add some warmth, try combining this rose with orange, a color with enough puckish energy to match the intensity of 'Veilchenblau'.

Opposite: 'Cécile Brünner' rose has been gracing gardens since it was introduced in 1881. Clusters of pastel-pink thimble-sized buds open into small, perfectly formed blooms. Soft, and sweet in fragrance, the flowers stand out against the dark green leaves on a 3-foot rounded bush. **Above:** Of all the flowering plants with spirelike blooms, foxgloves are often considered the easiest to grow. They're great for the back of the border or in a mass all by themselves. This cluster of dark violet to light pink foxgloves makes a colorful display. **Left:** This dramatic container design dares to combine bright yellow marigolds, chartreuse sweet potato vine, and yellow celosia with magenta petunias and hot pink zinnias. In the background, magenta is repeated in the old-fashioned cottage annual love-lies-bleeding and the perennial phlox.

Magenta Roses

'Russell's Cottage'

'Veilchenblau'

'Mrs. B. R. Cant'

'Rosarie del Hay'

'Madame Isaac Pereire'

'Magnifica'

'Intrigue'

'Deep Purple'

'Paradise'

'Falstaff'

'Noble Antony'

'Reine des Violettes'

'Rose de Rescht'

'Tess of the d'Urbervilles'

'Purple Heart'

Magenta Shrubs

Beautyberry: *Callicarpa bodinieri* 'Profusion', 'Early Amethyst'

Butterfly bush: *Buddleia davidii* 'Royal Red'

Crape myrtle: *Lagerstroemia* 'Wichita'

Rose of sharon: *Hibiscus syriacus* 'Violet Satin'

Rhododendron: *Rhododendron carolinianum* x *dauricum* 'P.J.M.'

Kurume azalea: *Rhododendron* 'Hinodedgiri'

Girard azalea: *Rhododendron* 'Renee Michelle'

Encore azalea: *Rhododendron* 'Autumn Amethyst'

Camellia: *Camellia sasanqua* 'Shishi Gashira', *C. japonica* 'Mathotiana Rubra'

Lilac: *Syringa* 'Pocahontas'

Oleander: *Nerium oleander* 'Hot Pink'

Bougainvillea: *Bougainvillea* 'Sanderiana'

Yesterday-today-and-tomorrow shrub: *Brunfelsia pauciflora*

Chinese witch hazel: *Loropetalum chinense* 'Plum Delight'

Above: Each spring my 'Russell's Cottage' rose delights me with its fragrant flowers. **Right:** American beautyberry produces tight clusters of berrylike drupes. The bright flowers of ironweed (*Vernonia*) also stand out in the late-summer landscape. **Opposite:** This cut-flower bouquet of magenta blooms includes 'Versailles Carmine' cosmos, 'Benary's Giant Purple' zinnia, 'Magnus' coneflower, 'Bouquet Purple' dianthus, 'Cramer's Burgundy' cockscomb (*Celosia cristata*) and 'Summer Bouquet' Obedient plant (*Physostegia virginiana*).

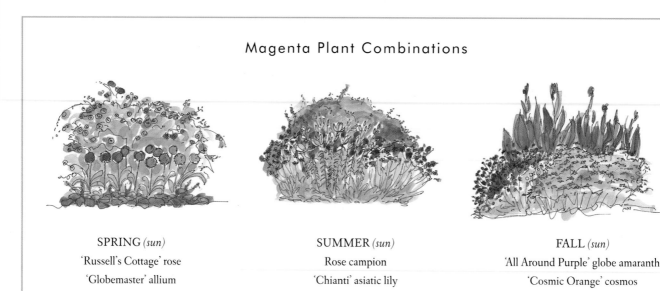

Magenta Plant Combinations

SPRING *(sun)*	SUMMER *(sun)*	FALL *(sun)*
'Russell's Cottage' rose	Rose campion	'All Around Purple' globe amaranth
'Globemaster' allium	'Chianti' asiatic lily	'Cosmic Orange' cosmos
'Palace Purple' heuchera	'Rosy Glow' barberry	'Black Knight' canna

Above: Magenta's dark side is beautifully represented in the foliage of this smoke-tree 'Velvet Cloak' (*Cotinus coggygria*). Some varieties of smoketree have deeply hued leaves in the spring that eventually turn green, but cultivars such as 'Velvet Cloak' retain their deep magenta color throughout most of the summer.

The cool color directory lists several magenta annual and perennial plants for you to consider, but there are also some great-looking shrubs that will supply a nice punch of color, including rhododendron 'Roseum elegans' in the north and crape myrtles 'Wichita' in the south.

Magenta needs to be combined with colors of different intensities to be noticed. So when you want to push your color scheme in the cool direction, it is best to choose either a lighter or darker shade of pink, purple, or lavender to complement the magenta. Gray and glaucous green foliage are also colors that resonate well with magenta.

While magenta does blend easily with other cool colors, that doesn't mean that you have to turn your back on warm hues. Various shades of magenta make an exciting combination with orange, an equal amount of purple, and a splash of yellow. For a little zest, add a pinch of chartreuse. In a supporting capacity, magenta adds depth and intensity to pink, blue, and lavender. It's also a great color bridge to bring pink into fall's tapestry. The hint of blue carried in magenta is just enough to make a successful color connection between pink, orange, and the reds of autumn.

As you explore the deeper tones of magenta, you will discover plum, and eventually plum-black, magenta's darkest incarnation. If you've ever found yourself struggling with how to use deep colors, such as plum, burgundy, or mahogany, it helps to trace them back to their parent colors. For instance, if you start with plum-black, and then lighten the color a step, that leads you to plum; a step lighter is magenta; and then medium pink. Pairing dark colors with hues that coordinate with the parent colors is always a safe bet.

COOL COLORS

PLANT DIRECTORY

BLUE   LAVENDER TO PURPLE   PINK   MAGENTA

PLANT NAME	QUICK FACTS	DESCRIPTION
Anise Hyssop *Agastache x hybrida* 'Blue Fortune'	Lavender-blue flowers Perennial (Z 5–9) H 3'; S	Long-flowering spikes with fragrant minty foliage bloom all summer on drought and heat tolerant plant. Needs good drainage.
Bachelor's Button, Cornflower *Centaurea cyanus* 'Florist Blue Boy', 'Jubilee Gem'	Deep lavender blue Annual H 24–30"; S	Upright plants with glaucous foliage and thistle-like flowers in spring to early summer. Best in cool temperatures. In mild climates sow seed in fall for spring bloom.
Balloon Flower *Platycodon grandiflorus* 'Fuji Blue'. Also try: 'Sentimental Blue'	Deep blue to violet-blue flowers Perennial (Z 4–9) H 24"; S–PS	This compact selection doesn't need staking and has novel inflated buds that open to 2¹⁄₂" star-shaped blooms. For floriferous dwarf, try 'Sentimental Blue', 6–8".
Bluebonnets, Lupines *Lupinus polyphyllus* x 'The Governor'	Dark blue and white flowers Perennial (Z 4–8) H 30–36"; S–PS	Gorgeous majestic hybrid lupine with bi-colored pea-like flowers on long spikes in early summer. Blooms best in northern climates with sunny days and cool nights. Best in masses.
Borage *Borago officinalis*	Blue flowers Perennial (Z 8–10) usually grown as annual H 18–36"; S–PS	Bushy edible herb with coarse, hairy foliage and clusters of beautiful star-shaped flowers. Best when direct seeded. Prefers moist, well-drained soil.
Bush Violet *Browallia speciosa* 'Blue Bells'	Blue flowers Annual H 9–12"; S–PS	Attractive plant with abundant blooms performs best in cool northern climates. Can be enjoyed as a cool-season annual, spring or fall, elsewhere.
Cape Leadwort *Plumbago auriculata* 'Imperial Blue'	Sky-blue flowers Perennial (Z 8–10) H 1–3'	Evergreen perennial shrub grown as an annual in most of the country. Blooms continuously in phlox-like clusters on upright, arching stems unfazed by heat and humidity.
Chinese Forget-Me-Not *Cynoglossum amabile* 'Blue Showers'. Also try: 'Firmament'	Sky-blue flowers Annual H 24–30"; S	Beautiful airy sprays of ¹⁄₄" flowers bloom late spring–early summer. Treat as cool-season annual as it declines in heat. 'Firmament' is dwarf variety, 15".
Columbine *Aquilegia x caerulea* 'Origami Blue and White'. Also try: 'Songbird Blue Jay', 'Songbird Blue Bird	Bi-colored blue and white flowers Perennial (Z 4–8) H 14–16"; PS	Hybrids of Rocky Mountain columbine are short-lived but charming with fernlike leaves and "spurred" spring blooms. 'Origami' blooms first year from seed. "Songbird" has large flowers on taller plants 24–30".
Delphinium *Delphinium belladonna* 'Bellamosum', 'Cliveden Beauty'. Also try: *D. grandiflorum* 'Blue Mirror', *D.* x 'Pacific Giants Blue Bird'	Light blue to deep blue flowers Perennial (Z 3–7) H 4'; S–PS	Belladonna hybrids provide beautiful blue shades on strong slender stems. Delphiniums, intolerant of hot climates, are often grown as fall-planted cool-season annuals. 'Blue Mirror' compact (24"). 'Blue Bird' is 5–6'.
Dwarf Morning Glory *Convolvulus tricolor* 'Blue Ensign'. Also try: *C. sabatius* 'Baby Moon' (aka *C. mauritanicus*)	Royal-blue flowers with white and yellow throats Annual H 8–12"; S	Free-flowering annual with compact trailing habit and flashy unique blooms. 'Baby Moon' smothers trailing stems with lavender-blue blooms. Good in containers.

BORAGE

BLUE-EYED GRASS

PLANT NAME	QUICK FACTS	DESCRIPTION
False Indigo *Baptisia australis*	Indigo blue flowers Perennial (Z 3–9) H 3–4'; S–PS	Long-blooming legume family member has upright vase shape and sweet pea–shaped flowers. Does not transplant easily.
Floss Flower *Ageratum houstonianum* 'Leilani Blue'. Also try: 'Neptune Blue'	Blue flowers Annual H 14–16"; S–PS	Masses of fluffy flowers with threadlike petals bloom in summer on full bushy plant. Needs fertile, moist soil. 'Neptune Blue'—dwarf (6–8") mounding variety.
Forget-Me-Not *Myosotis sylvatica* 'Bobo Blue', 'Victoria Indigo Blue'. Also try: *M. scorpiodes*; *M.* x 'Bluesylva'	Blue flowers Perennial (Z 5–8) H 6–10"; S–PS	Heavy bloomers with mounds of delicate foliage and dainty clusters of sweet-scented flowers in spring.
Grape hyacinths *Muscari armeniacum*. Also try: *M. armeniacum* 'Cantab', 'Saffier'; *M. aucheri* 'Blue Magic', *M.* 'Valerie Finnis'	Cobalt blue flowers Perennial (Z 4–8) H 6"; S–PS	Fall-planted bulb produces bloom spikes early to mid-spring resembling grape bunches. Prolific naturalizer. Many good blue *M. armeniacum* cultivars. 'Valerie Finnis'—unique light blue flowers.
Heartleaf Brunnera, Alkanet *Brunnera macrophylla*. Also try: 'Jack Frost'	Blue flowers Perennial (Z 3–8) H 12"; PS–Sh	Moisture-loving plant with large heart-shaped leaves and tiny flower clusters in spring. Needs protection from sun. 'Jack Frost' also offers silvery foliage.
Jacob's Ladder *Polemonium caeruleum*. Also try: *P. boreale* 'Heavenly Habit'	Blue flowers Perennial (Z 3–7) H 18–24"; S–PS	Spring-blooming flower clusters held above delicate leaflets that portray a ladder effect along stems. Not good southern plants. Fragrant 'Heavenly Habit' compact (12") with yellow eye.
Larkspur *Consolida ambigua* 'Giant Imperial Blue Bell'	Azure blue flowers Annual H 2–3'; S–PS	Antique variety has spires of flowers that bloom spring and early summer. Cool season annual can be planted in fall in mild areas for spring bloom.
Lily-of-the-Nile *Agapanthus* 'Ellamae'. Also try: 'Elaine', 'Storm Cloud', 'Peter Pan'	Violet-blue flowers Perennial (Z 8–11) H 5–6'; S–PS	Tender perennial from bulb produces clumps of graceful, strap-like foliage and in summer globes of bell-shaped flowers. Good container plants. 'Peter Pan' is dwarf (16") with narrow leaves.
Lobelia *Lobelia erinus* 'Crystal Palace'. Also try: 'Cambridge Blue'	Dark blue flowers Annual H 4–6"; S–PS	Low, trailing plants smothered in blooms all season where summers are cool. In hot climates site in partial shade for longer performance. 'Cambridge Blue' has sky-blue flowers.
Love-in-a-Mist *Nigella damescena* 'Miss Jekyll Blue'	Lavender to sky-blue flowers Maroon-striped seedpods Annual H 12–18"; S	Cool-season heirloom, often grown as novelty, produces semi-double flowers with ragged edges and a collar of feathery pinnately compound leaves. Seedpods can be dried for winter bouquets.
Monkshood *Aconitum napellus*. Also try: *Aconitum carmichaelii* 'Arendsii'	Blue flowers Perennial (Z 3–7) H 3–4'; PS	Stately plant with deeply lobed leaves and late summer blooms. Needs moist soils. 'Arendsii' is later flowering variety with deep blue flowers and compact (3') growth.

BLUE | COOL COLORS

HYDRANGEA 'NIKKO BLUE'   GENTIAN SAGE   GRAPE HYACINTH

PLANT NAME	QUICK FACTS	DESCRIPTION
Morning Glory *Ipomoea tricolor* 'Heavenly Blue'. Also try: *I. nil* 'Flying Saucers'	Sky-blue flowers with white throat Annual H 10'; S	Vigorous growth, abundant flowers and heart-shaped leaves have made this variety popular since the 1930s. For unusual blue and white striped 5" flowers, grow 'Flying Saucers'.
Pansy *Viola x wittrockiana* 'Crystal Bowl True Blue'. Also try: 'Icicle Clear Blue'	Medium blue flowers Annual H 6–8"; S–PS	Cold-hardy annual planted in fall or spring provides masses of 2–3" clear blue blooms on compact plant. 'Icicle' pansies are bred to survive harsh northern winters if fall-planted.
Peach-Leaved Bellflower *Campanula persicifolia* 'Telham Beauty'	Violet blue flowers Perennial (Z 3–9) H 2–3'; S–PS	Bell-shaped 3" blooms appear in summer on unbranched stems. Bellflowers need good drainage and struggle in areas with combination heat and humidity.
Plumbago *Ceratostigma plumbaginoides*	Blue flowers Perennial (Z 5–9) H 6–12"; S–PS	Creeping semi-woody perennial with dark green diamond-shaped leaves and 1" blooms occurring from mid-summer to fall. Makes a good, fast-growing ground cover.
Quamash *Camassia cusickii*. Also try: *C. quamash* 'Blue Melody'	Pale wisteria-blue flowers Perennial (Z 4–8) H 24–30"; S–PS	Northwest native with upright flowering racemes and long, narrow foliage. Needs moist soil. 'Blue Melody' is 15" with darker blue flowers and variegated foliage.
Salvia *Salvia nemorosa* 'Blue Hill'. Also try: *S. guaranitica* 'Black and Blue', *S. uliginosa, S. farinacea* 'Victoria Blue'	True blue flowers Perennial (Z 5–9) H 2'; S	Long-flowering spikes over compact foliage. Best with moisture and cool nights. Less hardy (Z 7) are 'Victoria Blue' with violet-blue flowers; *S. uliginosa* (4') with light blue blooms; 'Black and Blue' (3') with dark blue flowers with black calyxes.
Spanish Bluebells, Wood Hyacinths *Hyacinthoides hispanica* 'Excelsior'. Also try: English Bluebells (*H. non-scripta*)	Blue-violet flowers with marine blue mid-veins Perennial (Z 3–8) H 12–15"; S–PS	Fall-planted bulb produces strap-like foliage and strong stems of pendent flowers. Strong naturalizer and good in woodland settings. Fragrant *H. non-scripta* best in cool climates (Z 5–7).
Spiked Speedwell *Veronica spicata* 'Goodness Grows', 'Royal Candles', 'Sunny Border Blue'. Also try: *V. peduncularis* 'Georgia Blue', *V.* x 'Blue Reflection', *V.* 'Waterperry Blue'	Lavender-blue to dark blue flowers Perennial (Z 4–8) H 14–24"; S–PS	Long-blooming heat-tolerant selections flower late-spring through early summer on upright spreading stems. 'Waterperry', 'Blue Reflection', 'Georgia Blue' are creeping varieties.
Spotted Lungwort *Pulmonaria saccharata* 'Mrs. Moon'	Pink buds age to deep blue Perennial (Z 3–7) H 12"; PS–Sh	Perennial brightens up shade with handsome silver-spotted leaves and spring blooms. Needs shade and good drainage.
Virginia Bluebells *Mertensia virginica*	Pink flowers mature to purplish blue Perennial (Z 3–8) H 18–24"; PS–Sh	Sprays of nodding trumpet-shaped flowers bloom on upright stems with glaucous leaves several weeks in spring. Plants then go dormant. Over time forms large clumps.
Willow Blue Star *Amsonia taebernaemontana*	Light blue flowers Perennial (Z 3–9) H 2–3'; S–PS	Star-shaped 1/2" flowers are held terminally in clusters atop upright stems for 2–3 weeks in spring. Rarely reblooms but willow-like foliage is attractive glossy green.

QUICK FACTS COLOR DESCRIPTION: **Z** = Zone, **H** = Height, **S** = Sun, **PS** = Partial Sun or Partial Shade, **Sh** = Shade

PLANT NAME	QUICK FACTS	DESCRIPTION
Aster *Aster novae-angliae* 'Purple Dome'. Also try: *A.* 'Hella Lacy', *A. novi-belgii* 'Professor Kippenburg'	Purple flowers with yellow centers Perennial (Z 4–8) H 24–30"; S	Compact growth habit makes 'Purple Dome' one of the best New England asters. For larger plant try 'Hella Lacy' 3–4'. 'Prof. Kippenburg', 18" tall, has lavender flowers.
Beardtongue *Penstemon* 'Sour Grapes'. Also try: *P. smallii* 'Violet Dusk'	Pale purple flowers with white throats. Perennial (Z 7–9) H 24–30"; S–PS	Numerous penstemon species and hybrids exist. Basal evergreen leaves produce unbranched spikes with tiers of bell-shaped flowers in summer. 'Violet Dusk' hardy Z 6–8.
Blue Flag Iris *Iris versicolor.* Also try: Southern Blue Flag, (*I. virginica*)	Lavender to blue-violet flowers Perennial (Z 3–8) H 2–3'; S–PS	Stout, leafy native of the northern U.S. has 3" blooms in early summer. Usually found in or near water and in the garden prefers moist soil.
Catmint *Nepeta faassenii* 'Six Hills Giant'	Lavender flowers Perennial (Z 3–9) H 2–3'; S–PS	Vigorous, mounding plant with attractive foliage of small-toothed leaves and a profusion of flowers in spring and summer. Great for edging.
Clustered Bellflower *Campanula glomerata* 'Joan Elliot'	Purple flowers Perennial (Z 3–8) H 1–3'; S–PS	Stout, upright, summer-bloomer with dense terminal clusters of 1" flowers. Plants spread to form clumps. Bellflowers are happiest in cool climates.
Cupflower *Nierembergia frutescens* 'Purple Robe'	Dark violet-blue flowers Annual H 6"; S–PS	Numerous cup-shaped flowers produced all spring and summer on slender stems with linear 1" leaves. At its best as a container plant.
Delphinium *Delphinium x elatum* 'Pacific Giants', 'Black Knight'	Deep purple flowers with black bee (center) Perennial (Z 3–7) H 4–5'; S	Delphiniums, intolerant of hot climates, are often grown as fall-planted cool-season annual. In south set out plants in fall. This tall variety may need staking.
Fan Flower *Scaevola aemula* 'Purple Fan', 'Whirlwind Blue', 'New Wonder'	Purple flowers Annual H 1'; S	Hybrid of Australian native with oblong, fleshy 2" leaves and trailing stems. Solitary 1" fan-shaped flowers in leaf axils bloom all summer. Needs good drainage.
Golden Dewdrop, Sky Flower *Duranta erecta* 'Sapphire Showers'	Dark lavender flowers with white stripe Perennial (Z 8–11) H 2–4'; S	Shrubby evergreen blooms for weeks or months in summer and fall. Arching stems hold multiple racemes of flowers. Where frosts are late, forms clusters of golden berries.
Hyacinth *Hyacinthus orientalis* 'Peter Stuyvesant'	Dark purple flowers Perennial (Z 5–9) H 8–12"; S–PS	Spring-flowering bulb, planted in fall, produces a thick, formal-looking spike densely packed with fragrant flowers. This variety is one of the darkest purple.
Ladybells *Adenophora confusa*	Purplish-blue flowers Perennial (Z 3–8) H 36"; S–PS	Drought-tolerant ladybells selection with fragrant, nodding, bell-shaped 1" flowers symmetrically arranged on many tall stems.

LAVENDER TO PURPLE | COOL COLORS

PLANT NAME	QUICK FACTS	DESCRIPTION
Larkspur *Consolida ambigua* 'Giant Imperial Blue Spire'. Also try: 'Giant Imperial Lilac Spire'	Deep purple flowers Annual H 30–48"; S	Antique variety has spires of flowers that bloom spring and early summer. Cool season annual can be planted in fall in mild areas for spring bloom.
Lavender *Lavandula* x *intermedia* 'Provence'. Also try: *Lavandula stoechas* 'Otto Quast'	Lavender-blue flowers Perennial (Z 6–9) H 2–3'; S	This hardy hybrid lavender is somewhat more rot-resistant in humid climates than English lavender. 'Otto Quast', a Spanish lavender, also tolerant but less cold hardy (Z 7–10).
Lobelia *Lobelia* x *gerardii* 'Vedrariensis'	Violet-blue flowers Perennial (Z 7–10) H 2–4'; S–PS	Robust but short-lived perennial produces showy flower spikes in mid- to late summer. Like other cardinal flower relatives, it needs moist soil.
Monkshood *Aconitum cammarum* 'Bressingham Spire'	Violet-blue flowers Perennial (Z 4–8) H 36"; S–Sh	This variety has deeply cut leaves, stocky habit, and helmet-shaped flowers on dense racemes. Enjoys fertile, slightly acidic soil. All plant parts are poisonous.
Nemesia *Nemesia* x *hybrida* 'Blueberry Sachet' *Nemesia fruticans* 'Blue Bird'	Violet-blue flowers Tender perennial (Z 9–10) H 10–12"; S–PS	Cultivar of South African native with spatula-like leaves and 1/2–1" fragrant flowers that bloom in clusters. Prefers moist soil and cooler temperatures.
Pansy *Viola* x *wittrockiana* 'Accord Clear Purple', 'Purple Rain'. Also try: Johnny-Jump-ups, *V. cornuta* 'Penny Deep Blue'	Purple flowers Annual H 4–8"; S–PS	Cold-hardy annual planted in fall or spring provides masses of 2–3" blooms. Violas with smaller, more numerous blooms, are more weather tolerant.
Persian Shield *Strobilanthes dyeranus*	Bronze-green leaf with iridescent violet sheen Annual H 2–4'; P–PS	Upright soft-stemmed shrub grown for its 6–9" lanceolate opposite leaves. Warm temperatures and sun produce best leaf color.
Pincushion Flower *Scabiosa columbaria* 'Butterfly Blue'	Lavender flowers Perennial (Z 4–8) H 12–15"; S	Gray-green basal foliage and 2" round cushioned-shaped flowers bloom prolifically from spring to fall, slowing down only in hottest weather.
Purple Plectranthus *Plectranthus* 'Mona Lavender'	Lavender flowers Annual H 2–6'; S–PS	Shrubby, upright plant with aromatic leaves earns its keep in late summer when short days signal multiple flower spikes to bloom for several weeks.
Russian Sage *Perovskia atriplicifolia*	Lavender flowers Perennial (Z 5–9) H 3–5'; S	Narrow dissected leaves, waxy stems, and panicles of long-blooming 1/4" tubular flowers make this a summer-long asset in the garden. Needs well-drained soil in winter.
Salvia *Salvia splendens* 'Salsa Purple', 'Salsa Light Purple'	Light to dark purple flowers Annual H 12–14"; S–PS	Compact hybrid of Brazilian native with dark green leaves and densely arranged whorls of flowers on numerous spikes. Blooms dependably summer and fall.
Siberian Iris *Iris sibirica* 'Silver Edge'. Also try: 'Coronation Anthem'	Light lavender and deep lavender flowers Perennial (Z 4–9) H 26–30"; S–PS	Graceful, beardless Siberian iris have narrow, grasslike foliage and prefer moist, slightly acid soils. This older variety's bloom has white edge. 'Coronation Anthem' is deep blue-purple.

QUICK FACTS COLOR DESCRIPTION: **Z** = Zone, **H** = Height, **S** = Sun, **PS** = Partial Sun or Partial Shade, **Sh** = Shade

DWARF CRESTED IRIS

LADYBELLS

AMERICAN BASKETFLOWER

PLANT NAME	QUICK FACTS	DESCRIPTION
Solitary Clematis *Clematis integrifolia*	Blue to purple flowers Perennial (Z 3–7) H 3–5'; S–PS	Non-vining clematis with numerous thin stems that need support. Prolific bloomer for several weeks in spring/summer.
Spiderwort *Tradescantia* x *andersoniana* 'Concord Grape'. Also try: 'Zwanenburg Blue'	Bluish-purple flowers with blue-green foliage Perennial (Z 4–9) H 15–24"; S–PS	Improved cultivar of native plant has frosty, blue, grass-like foliage and many 1¹⁄₂" flowers in early summer. Needs moisture and afternoon shade in hot climates.
Spreading/Cascading Petunias *Petunia hybrida* 'Ramblin' Nu Blue', 'Blue Wave', 'Surfinia Violet', 'Cascadia Improved Charlie'	Deep blue purple flowers Annual H 6"; S–PS	Low-growing petunias with spreading or cascading habit from 1–4' are great in containers or in beds for a ground-cover effect.
Stokes Aster *Stokesia laevis* 'Blue Danube'. Also try: 'Klaus Jelitto', 'Peachie's Pick'	Lavender-blue flowers Perennial (Z 5–9) H 12–18"; S–PS	Native plant hybrid with neat mounds of foliage and 3–4" cornflower-like blooms appearing in early to midsummer. Needs good winter drainage.
Summer Snapdragon *Angelonia angustifolia* 'Carita Lavender', 'Carita Purple', 'AngelMist Lavender'	Lavender to purple flowers Annual H 18"; S	Upright summer-long bloomer, with a bushy, branching habit, provides multiple spikes covered with small orchid-like blossoms. Pinch back to keep neat.
Tall Verbena, Verbena-on-a-Stick *Verbena bonariensis.* Also try: *V. rigida*	Lavender flowers Perennial (Z 7–9) H 3–6'; S	Upright South American native with tall, slender stems that end with numerous flower clusters that almost appear suspended in midair. Blooms all spring and summer. *V. rigida* similar but more compact.
Verbena *Verbena canadensis* 'Homestead Purple'. Also try: 'Rapunzel Light Lavender'	Deep purple flowers Perennial (Z 7–11) H 6–10"; S	'Homestead Purple' is a heat- and drought-tolerant, early-flowering verbena with vigorous, spreading habit and multitude of vibrant blooms. 'Rapunzel Light Lavender' is annual with good disease resistance and long bloom.
Violet Sage *Salvia superba* 'May Night'. Also try: *Salvia* x 'Indigo Spires'; Mexican Sage *S. leucantha*	Violet-blue flowers Perennial (Z 4–9) H 18"; S	Compact hybrid with numerous flower spikes in late spring–early summer. Performs best with good moisture and cool nights. 'Indigo Spires' and *S. leucantha* (Z 7) are taller and peak late summer through fall.
Weeping Lantana *Lantana montevidensis*	Lavender flowers Perennial (Z 8–11) H 6–12"; S–PS	Spreading plant produces profusion of flower umbels summer through fall. Heat, wind, and drought-tolerant.
Wishbone Flower *Torenia fournieri* hybrid 'Purple Moon', 'Summer Wave'. Also try: *T. fournieri* 'Duchess Deep Blue'	Dark purple flowers Annual H 6–12"; S–PS	Vegetative hybrid with trailing habit and sun/heat tolerance provides beautiful color spring through fall. 'Duchess Deep Blue' similar with upright mounding habit.
Woodland Phlox *Phlox divaricata* 'May Breeze', 'Chattahooche'	Lavender to purple flowers Perennial (Z 4–9) H 12–15"; PS–Sh	Native plant with fragrant spring flowers is good companion for dogwoods and redbuds. Best grown in rich, well-drained soil with filtered light.

BEE BALM 'MARSHALL'S DELIGHT'

SAUCER MAGNOLIA

PLANT NAME	QUICK FACTS	DESCRIPTION
Anemone *Anemone x hybrida* 'September Charm'. Also try: *Anemone tomentosa* 'Robustissima'	Rose-pink flowers Perennial (Z 5–9) H 30"; S–PS	Spreading plant with attractive grape-leaf-shaped foliage and airy flowers that bloom late summer to fall. Plants look their best in moist, humus-rich soil.
Argyranthemum *Argyranthemum frutecens* 'Comet Pink'	Light pink flower with yellow center Annual H 16–20"; S	A good season extender for cool-season flowers through spring and early summer. Upright habit with daisy-shaped blooms.
Asiatic Lily *Lilium* Asiatic hybrid 'Chianti'. Also try: *L.* trumpet hybrid, 'Pink Perfection'; *L.* Oriental hybrid 'Le Reve'	Champagne pink with darker pink throat Perennial (Z 4–8) H 3–4'; S	Easy-to-grow bulb can be planted in fall or spring for large star-shaped blooms on upright stems in early summer. For larger flowers on 4–6' stems, plant 'Pink Perfection'. 'Le Reve' has clear, pink fragrant blooms.
Astilbe *Astilbe simplicifolia* 'Sprite', 'Hennie Graafland'. Also try: *A. x arendsii* 'Peach Blossom'	Shell-pink flowers Perennial (Z 4–9) H 12–16"; S–PS	Low-growing astilbe for front of border best used en masse for ground-cover effect. Produces long-lasting feathery plumes in midsummer. Prefers rich moist, well-drained soil. Needs shade in South. 'Peach Blossom' is earlier bloomer, 20–40" tall.
Bee Balm *Monarda* 'Marshall's Delight'. Also try: 'Petite Wonder'	Hot pink flowers Perennial (Z 4–9) H 36"; S–PS	Highly mildew-resistant variety with dense flower clusters on top of upright stems with aromatic foliage. Spreads in moist soils. 'Petite Wonder' is a disease-resistant dwarf, 10" tall.
Begonia *Begonia* x 'Ina Mae'. Also try: *B.* 'Dragonwing Pink', *B. grandis*	Pink flowers Annual H 18"; S–PS	Hard-to-find begonia with sturdy upright growth, glossy dark-green leaves and pendulous flower clusters. "Dragonwings" are similar performers and easier to find. *B. grandis* is perennial Z 6–10.
Boltonia *Boltonia asteroides* 'Pink Beauty'	Pale pink flowers Perennial (Z 4–9) H 4–5'; S	Showy pale pink aster-type flowers bloom in September on clean silver bluish foliage. Tolerant of dry to moist soils. Full sun needed to maintain upright stature. Cut back in early to midsummer for a less lanky habit. May need support.
Bush Peony *Paeonia* 'Sarah Bernhardt' Also try: 'Mons Jules Elie', 'Abalone Pearl'	Rose-pink flowers Perennial (Z 3–8) H 34"; S–PS	Hardy, long-lived peonies are ideal for cold climates but less so in south. 'Mons Jules Elie' and 'Abalone Pearl' recommended as heat-tolerant pinks.
Caladium *Caladium bicolor* 'Florida Sweetheart' Also try: 'Florida Roselight'	Deep pink and green leaves Annual H 12"; PS–Sh	Improved hybrid caladium with disease resistance and vigorous growth on a compact plant. Provides lush colorful foliage all summer. 'Florida Roselight' is lighter pink.
Cardinal Flower *Lobelia* 'Cotton Candy', *Lobelia speciosa* 'Fan Deep Rose'	Soft pink-lavender flowers Perennial (Z 4–9) H 28"; S–PS	Flat rosette of foliage topped in late summer and early fall with a 2' tall flower spike of large blooms. Enjoys a moist position in the flowerbed. 'Fan Deep Rose' has spikes of large, deep pink-rose tubular flowers that bloom from seed the first year.
Cheddar Pinks *Dianthus* 'Bewitched'. Also try: *D. gratianopolitanus* 'Bath's Pink'	Light pink flowers with magenta eye Perennial (Z 5–8) H 8–12"; S	Compact cultivar with silvery evergreen linear foliage blooms longer in spring and performs better in heat than old varieties. For great fragrance try 'Bath's Pink'.

QUICK FACTS COLOR DESCRIPTION: **Z** = Zone, **H** = Height, **S** = Sun, **PS** = Partial Sun or Partial Shade, **Sh** = Shade

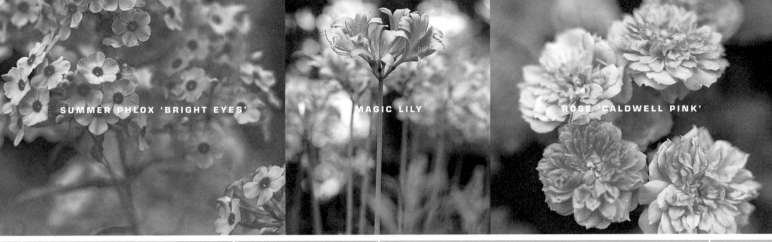

SUMMER PHLOX 'BRIGHT EYES'   MAGIC LILY   ROSE 'CALDWELL PINK'

PLANT NAME	QUICK FACTS	DESCRIPTION
Clematis *Clematis x jackmanii* 'Comtesse de Bouchaud'. Also try: 'Hagley Hybrid'	Pink flowers with yellow stamens Perennial (Z 4–9) H 6–10'; S–PS	Large-flowered hybrid clematis are colorful vines that need support. This carefree variety has profusion of satiny flowers. 'Hagley Hybrid' has shell-pink petals and chocolate stamens.
Coleus *Coleus hybrida* 'Old Lace'	Pink-rose foliage with green margins Annual H 8–12", S–PS	Small lace-like foliage is a bright pink-rose color with green margins. The brilliant colors explode in sunny locations. Flower buds should be pinched off as soon as they develop. Avoid overwatering or poorly drained soil.
Columbine *Aquilegia caerulea* 'Origami Rose and White'	Deep pink and white flowers Perennial (Z 6–11) H 18–36"; S–PS	Lacy foliage and beautiful flowers give columbines a fairylike, woodland-glen quality. 'Origami Rose and White' has an extended bloom time longer than the usual 2–3 weeks. Thrives in a rich, moist, well-drained soil. Also good in containers.
Coral Bells *Heuchera* 'Strawberry Candy'	Pink panicles of flowers Perennial (Z 4–9) H 9–16" (foliage); S–PS	Clump-forming perennial with green leaves marbled in silver. Large, open, airy panicles appear in late spring to early summer on slender, wiry stems rising well above the foliage mound (28" tall).
Cosmos *Cosmos bipinnatus* 'Sonata Pink'. Also try: 'Gazebo Pink', 'Versailles Pink'	Pink flowers with yellow centers Annual H 20"; S	Compact, free-flowering cultivar of graceful, airy annual has feathery foliage and 4" daisies in summer. 'Gazebo Pink' and 'Versailles Pink' are taller varieties good for the back of the border (3–4').
Culver's Root *Veronicastrum virginicum* 'Fascination'	Mauve to pink blooms Perennial (Z 3–8) H 3–4'; S	Striking candelabra-shaped plant with whorls of lance-shaped foliage and strong upright blooming stems in mid to late summer with iridescent lavender-pink sheen.
Daylily *Hemerocallis* 'Jolyene Nicole'. Also try: 'Janice Brown', 'Cherry Cheeks', 'Jedi Free Spirit', 'Siloam Double Classic'	Rose-pink flowers Perennial (Z 3–9) H 14"; S–PS	Adaptable daylilies have summer flowers that only last one day but come in clusters for several weeks. This variety has large blooms with pie-crust ruffling. 'Janice Brown' is 21" H and two-toned pink. 'Cherry Cheeks' (28") is deep pink with an orange throat. 'Jedi Free Spirit' is vigorous and trouble-free. 'Siloam Double Classic' has double flowers.
Egyptian Starflower *Pentas lanceolata* 'Butterfly Deep Pink'	Pink flowers Annual H 12–18"; S–PS	Vigorous heat-loving annual blooms profusely all summer with star-shaped flower clusters. Loved by butterflies. Adding lime helps *Pentas'* performance in acidic soil.
Fleece Flower Persicaria amplexicaulis 'Rosea'	Pink flowers Perennial (Z 6–8) H 4'; S–PS	In late summer to fall, 4–5" tapered spikes bloom over lush, prominently veined foliage. 'Rosea' spreads but, unlike some fleece flowers, is not invasive. Prefers ample moisture.
Geranium *Pelargonium x hortorum* 'Rocky Mountain Light Pink'. Also try: 'Maverick Pink', 'Orbit Pink'	Light pink flowers Annual H 14–16"; S–PS	Semi-double flowers in umbels held above foliage bloom all summer. Each orbicular-shaped leaf has a dark horseshoe-shaped zone. Vigorous plant with good heat tolerance.
Heath Aster *Aster ericoides* 'Pink Star'. Also try: *A. Novae-angliae* 'Alma Potschke'	Soft pink flowers Perennial (Z 4–10) H 2'; S–PS	Mounding, drought-tolerant Dutch selection of a U.S. wildflower is smothered in daisies in late summer to early fall. 'Alma Potschke' is 36" tall with vivid pink blooms.

MODERN PINK

ORIENTAL LILY 'STARGAZER'

COSMOS 'SONATA PINK'

PINK | COOL COLORS

PLANT NAME	QUICK FACTS	DESCRIPTION
Hibiscus *Hibiscus moscheutos* 'Disco Belle Pink'	Pink and white flower with red eye Perennial (Z 5–9) H 3'; S	A compact hardy hibiscus with multiple woody stems and numerous enormous flowers (8") throughout summer. Deciduous plant emerges late in spring.
Impatiens *Impatiens wallerana* 'Accent Deep Pink'	Deep pink flowers Annual H 12"; PS–Sh	One of the most popular bedding plants and invaluable for color in shade. This variety is a prolific bloomer all summer and fall.
Lantana *Lantana camara* 'Athens Rose'. Also try: 'Landmark Pink Dawn', 'Landmark Rose Glow'	Pink and yellow flowers Perennial (Z 7–11) H 3–4'; S	Tiny flowers in tight clusters resembling miniature nosegays bloom continuously in warm weather. Extremely heat and drought tolerant. 'Landmark Pink Dawn' and 'Landmark Rose Glow' are less hardy, compact (18–24") landscape cultivars that feature clusters of soft pink or rose flowers mixed with soft yellow.
Mandevilla Vine *Mandevilla x amoena* 'Alice du Pont'. Also try: *M. sanderi* 'Red Riding Hood'	Hot pink flowers Tropical perennial (Z 10–11) often grown as annual H 8–30'; S–PS	Fast-growing, woody climber flowers profusely and continuously with trumpet-shaped blooms all summer. This variety, with large oval leaves, is considered one of the best.
Mexican Evening Primrose *Oenothera berlandieri* 'Siskiyou'	Pale pink flowers Perennial (Z 4–8) H 6–8"; S–PS	Compact, slightly less-vigorous selection of invasive wildflower has 3", cup-shaped long-blooming flowers. Plant only in difficult soils where spreading will be welcome.
Mexican Hyssop *Agastache* 'Tutti-frutti'	Lavender pink flowers Perennial (Z 6–10) H 3–4'; S	Fragrant, gray-green foliage and foot-long flower spikes from early summer to frost attract hummingbirds to this cultivar.
Moss Rose *Portulaca grandiflora* 'Sundial Princess Pink', 'Yubi Summer Joy Pink'	Pink flowers Annual H 6", spread 12"; S	Fleshy, low-growing plant with brilliant rose-like flowers that thrive in hot, full-sun conditions. Blossoms open fully in bright light and close by mid-afternoon in hot weather. 'Sundial Princess Pink' resists closing and blooms with double 2" flowers in cooler, cloudier weather. 'Yubi Summer Joy Pink' does well in full sun hanging baskets.
Moss Verbena *Verbena x hybrida* 'Tapien Pink', 'Sissinghurst'	Pink flowers Perennial (Z 7–10) H 12–18"; S	Heat-tolerant moss verbenas have mildew-resistant fernlike foliage, as well as prolific, beautiful flower clusters spring through fall.
Nemesia *Nemesia fruticans* 'Compact Pink Innocence', 'Antique Rose Sachet'	Pink flowers Tender perennial (Z 9–10) often grown as annual H 10–12"; S–PS	Softly scented pink flowers. Plants perform best in cool gardens or partial shade in hot areas. Not drought-tolerant, so keep soil moist. 'Antique Rose Sachet' has rose and pink bicolor flowers.
Obedient Plant *Physostegia virginiana* 'Vivid'	Bright pink flowers Perennial (Z 3–9) H 20–24"; S–PS	Compact, later-blooming form of a vigorous spreading native plant. Snapdragon-like flowers in vertical rows on upright spikes bloom in early fall.
Old-Fashioned Bleeding Heart *Dicentra spectabilis*. Also try: *D.* 'Luxuriant'	Pink and white flowers Perennial (Z 3–9) H 2–4'; PS–Sh	Compound leaves and drooping chains of heart-shaped flowers emerge in early spring for several weeks in moist, cool conditions. Plants often go dormant in midsummer.

QUICK FACTS COLOR DESCRIPTION: **Z** = Zone, **H** = Height, **S** = Sun, **PS** = Partial Sun or Partial Shade, **Sh** = Shade

PURPLE CONEFLOWER

JAPANESE ANEMONE 'SEPTEMBER CHARM'

PLANT NAME	QUICK FACTS	DESCRIPTION
Pincushion Flower *Scabiosa columbaria* 'Pink Mist'	Pink flowers Perennial (Z 4–8) H 12–15"; S–PS	Gray-green basal foliage and 2" round cushioned-shaped flowers bloom prolifically from spring to fall, slowing down only in hottest weather.
Prairie Mallow *Sidalcea* 'Party Girl'. Also try: 'Elsie Heugh'	Bright pink flowers with white center Perennial (Z 5–9) H 36–42"; S	This hollyhock cousin produces vertical spikes of 1–2" flowers in mid to late summer. Moist, well-drained soil ensures long bloom. Performs best in cool climes. 'Elsie Heugh' is 30" with shell-pink flowers.
Rosebud Salvia *Salvia involucrata* 'Bethelli'. Also try: *S.* 'Mulberry Jam'	Deep rose-pink Perennial (Z 8–10) often grown as annual H 4–6'; S–PS	Also known as bulbous pink sage, as flowers terminate in a knob. Lax plants benefit from 1 or 2 pinches before they bloom in late summer. 'Mulberry Jam' is shorter (5') with more graceful flower spike.
Spider Flower *Cleome* 'Sparkler Blush'	Two-toned pink flowers Annual H 2–3'; S	New variety of an old-fashioned, unique flower has improved compact, bushy habit. Cleomes have palmate leaves on upright stems and large flower clusters with long, "spidery" stamens.
Stonecrop *Sedum spectabile* 'Brilliant', 'Neon'	Rose-pink flowers Perennial (Z 4–9) H 24"; S	Flattened clusters bloom over succulent foliage in late summer and last through fall. 'Neon' is superior variety with thicker, deeper-pink flower heads.
Summer Phlox *Phlox paniculata* 'Bright Eyes', 'Eva Cullum'. Also try: *P. maculata* 'Natascha'	Pink flowers with red eye Perennial (Z 4–8) H 30–36"; S	Tough perennial blooms in clusters at the tops of multiple stems from early to late summer. 'Bright Eyes' is fragrant, mildew-resistant variety. 'Natascha' is 24", with pink and white striped flowers.
Trailing Petunia *Calibrachoa* x *hybrida* 'Superbells Pink', 'Million Bells Trailing Pink'	Pink flowers Annual H 7–10"; S	Disease-resistant plants with prostrate growth habit and abundant small petunia-like flowers from spring to fall. Good cascader for baskets and containers.
Tulip *Tulipa* Darwin Hybrid 'Pink Impression'. Also try: 'Dreamland', 'Angelique'	Pink flowers flushed with rose Perennial bulbs (Z 3-7); treat as annuals in warm climates H 18-24"; S	Clusters of early-spring-blooming 'Pink Impression' tulips look like giant wine goblets in the border. 'Dreamland', a single late-season tulip, starts white with bright pink petal margins, and then pink expands, taking over most of the white. 'Angelique' has fully double strawberry- and cream-colored blooms.
Vinca, Periwinkle *Catharanthus roseus* 'Pink Cooler', 'Icy Pink Cooler', 'Pacifica Pink'	Pink to pastel pink flowers with a white eye Annual H 12–15"; S–PS	Compact plants with large 2" flowers clothed in glossy, green leaves blooming continuously in hot weather. These thrive in both humid and dry heat but are prone to disease in cool, wet soils.
Wand Flower *Gaura lindheimeri* 'Pink Fountain'. Also try: 'Siskiyou Pink' 'Karalee Petite Pink'	White flowers with pink blush Perennial (Z 6–9) H 2–3'; S	This selection of a tough adaptable Texas native has dense habit and increased lateral branching. Airy flowers at branch tips appear summer through fall.
Zinnia *Zinnia hybrida* 'Profusion Cherry'	Hot pink multi-petaled flowers Annual H 12–18"; S	Zesty color and round blooms are a long time favorite in flower borders. Blooms from summer to frost with deadheading. Medium height flowers are disease-resistant and excellent as cut flowers. Attracts butterflies.

PINK | COOL COLORS

ALLIUM 'PURPLE SENSATION'

ASTER 'SEPTEMBER RUBY'

BLOODLEAF PLANT

MAGENTA | COOL COLORS

PLANT NAME	QUICK FACTS	DESCRIPTION
Argyranthemum *Argyranthemum* 'Bright Carmine'	Carmine pink flowers with yellow centers Annual H 16–20″; S	A good season extender for cool season flowers through spring and early summer. Upright habit with daisy-shaped blooms.
Asiatic Lily *Lilium*, Asiatic hybrid, 'Cote d'Azur'. Also try: *L.* Oriental hybrid 'Acapulco'	Fuchsia flowers Perennial (Z 4–8) H 2–3′; S–PS	Easy-to-grow bulb can be planted in fall or spring for large star-shaped blooms on upright stems that flower in early summer. Compact variety good for containers. 'Acapulco' is a tall (4′), robust Oriental hybrid with reddish pink blooms.
Aster *Aster novae-angliae* 'September Ruby'. Also try: *A. dumosus* 'Winston Churchill', *A.* 'Alert'	Magenta red flowers Perennial (Z 4–8) H 2–4′; S	Prolific bloomer with strong stems and 1″ daisies blooms in fall. 'Winston Churchill' is more compact (18–24″) and earlier bloom (late summer). 'Alert' is 12″.
Astilbe *Astilbe chinensis* 'Visions'. Also try: 'Purple Candles'	Rose-purple flowers Perennial (Z 4–9) H 16″; S–PS	Compact, clump-forming cultivar with torch-like plumes and handsome, compound leaves. Astilbes need moisture and shade in hot climates. 'Purple Candles' is tall, bold cultivar (42″).
Bee Balm *Monarda* 'Raspberry Wine'	Violet flowers Perennial (Z 4–9) H 2–3′; S–PS	Dense clusters of tubular, two-lipped flowers atop vigorous, mildew-resistant native hybrid. Blooms late spring to summer. Spreads in moist soils.
Blazing Star *Liatris spicata* 'Floristan Violet'. Also try: 'Kobold'	Rosy-purple flowers Perennial (Z 3–9) H 3–4′; S	Native plant cultivar with small flowers covering erect stems tolerates heat, cold, drought, and poor soil. 'Kobold' similar but compact (24–30″).
Bloodleaf, Beefsteak Plant *Iresine herbstii*	Burgundy foliage with violet veins Annual H 12″; S–PS	Upright annual used in containers and bedding for its striking foliage colors rather than its flowers.
Bloody Cranesbill *Geranium sanguineum*. Also try: *G. psilostemon*	Magenta-pink flowers Perennial (Z 3–8) H 12″; S–PS	Blooms for 6–8 weeks in spring to early summer with numerous 1″ flowers over mound of finely divided foliage. Does well throughout country. *G. psilostemon* (Z 5–7) not for the south.
Burnet *Sanguisorba officinalis* 'Tanna'	Maroon flowers Perennial (Z 4–9) H 10″; S–PS	Dwarf, rhizomatous plant with pinnate basal leaves and bottle-brush flower spikes in late summer to fall. Needs moist, well-drained soil.
Cardinal Flower *Lobelia* 'Royal Fuchsia'	Violet flowers Perennial (Z 5–8) H 24″; S–PS	Lobelias are not long-lived perennials but provide striking color in mid- to late summer when other perennials are finished. This cultivar has fluorescent blossoms on strong, well-branched plants. Prefers moist, rich soil.
Celosia *Celosia spicata* 'Flamingo Purple'. Also try: *C. argentea cristata* 'Temple Bells Dark Rose', 'Chief Carmine'	Violet plumes Bronze foliage Annual H 3–4′; S	Tall annual with slender wheat-shaped flowers and erect bronze foliage has big impact at back of the summer border. *Celosia cristata* varieties have wavy flower crests giving cockscomb appearance.

QUICK FACTS COLOR DESCRIPTION: **Z** = Zone, **H** = Height, **S** = Sun, **PS** = Partial Sun or Partial Shade, **Sh** = Shade

PLANT NAME	QUICK FACTS	DESCRIPTION
Chinese Foxglove *Rehmannia elata*	Pink to violet flowers Biennial or short-lived perennial (Z 8–10) H 1½–3'; S–PS	Tall spikes of gloxinia-shaped flowers in late spring over basal rosette of veined, hairy leaves. Spreads by underground runners. Sometimes survives in Z 7.
Clematis *Clematis x jackmanii* 'Earnest Markham', 'Ville de Lyon'	Carmine flowers with beige stamens Perennial (Z 4–9) H 9'; S–PS	Two dependable old large-flowered hybrids bloom in late spring to early summer and often repeat. While clematis bloom well in sun, their roots prefer cool shade.
Coleus *Coleus hybrida* 'Stained Glassworks Trailing Plum', 'Swinging Linda'. Also Try: 'Garnet Robe'	Burgundy and violet leaves with gold borders Annual H 8–12"; S–PS	Vigorous hybrid of old-fashioned foliage plant has opposite leaves and square stems with a trailing habit. Good for containers and beds.
Common Foxglove *Digitalis purpurea.* Also try: *Digitalis purpurea* 'Camelot Rose'	Purple-pink flowers Biennial or short-lived perennial (Z 4–8) H 2–5'; S–PS	Short-lived European wildflower blooms its second year with numerous flowers on tall stems over basal rosette of foliage. 'Camelot Rose' is a new hybrid that blooms its first year.
Coral Bells *Heuchera micrantha* 'Palace Purple', 'Plum Pudding', 'Frosted Violet'	Dark burgundy foliage; white to pink flowers Perennial (Z 3–8) H 8–15"; PS–Sh	Native shade perennial cultivars with handsome dark rounded leaves provide interest even before dainty spring flowers appear.
Cordyline *Cordyline australis* 'Red Sensation'	Dark-purple foliage Perennial (Z 8–10) H 3–4'; S–PS	Moderately frost-hardy New Zealand native with dark ½" wide, 18" long leaves radiating out from a central stalk. Dramatic accent plant for beds and borders.
Creeping Thrift *Phlox subulata* 'Atropurpurea'. Also try: *P. stolonifera* 'Homefires'	Wine-red flowers Perennial (Z 2–9) H 4–6"; S	Spreading evergreen mats of stiff needle-shaped foliage obscured with flowers in spring. Needs well-drained soil. Good rock-garden plant or ground cover. 'Homefires' grows in partial shade.
Dahlia *Dahlia* 'Thomas Edison'	Violet purple flowers Perennial (Z 8–10) H 3'; S	Large (9") velvety blooms appear consistently late summer to fall from this tuber-grown plant. Looks best with fertilization, deadheading, and staking.
Dianthus *Dianthus* 'Amazon Neon Purple' Also try: 'Bouquet Purple'. *D. gratianopolitanus* 'Firewitch'	Magenta flowers Perennial (Z 5–9) sometimes grown as annual H 18–24"; S	New variety with mounded flower clusters blooms in spring but also repeats in summer and fall. 'Bouquet Purple' more "wispy" informal habit. 'Firewitch' compact (7").
Floss Flower *Ageratum houstonianum* 'Island Mist Magenta', 'Red Sea', 'Artist Purple'	Magenta flowers Annual H 18–24"; S–PS	Upright annual with dense tasseled flower clusters. Heat, humidity, and dry soil can hasten plant's decline. Seed can be started midsummer to replace spent plants.
Flowering Onion *Allium hollandicum* 'Purple Sensation'. Also try: drumstick allium, *A. sphaerocephalum*	Violet-purple Perennial (Z 4–8) H 24–30"; S–PS	Star-shaped florets clustered on 4–5" globes appear spring to early summer from fall-planted bulb. Mixes well with other flowers. *A. sphaerocephalon* (Z 5–8), with smaller flower, blooms later.

MAGENTA | COOL COLORS

MAGENTA | COOL COLORS

PLANT NAME	QUICK FACTS	DESCRIPTION
Gladiola *Gladiolus communis* subsp. *Byzantinus*	Magenta flowers Perennial (Z 6–10) H 2–3'; S	European species grown from a corm is hardier than more common African gladiolas. Sword-like leaves and tall spikes of $1^{1}/_{2}$" flowers appear in early summer.
Globe Amaranth *Gomphrena globosa* 'All-around Purple'. Also try: 'Gnome Purple'	Fuchsia flowers Annual H $1^{1}/_{2}$–2'; S	Tough plant throughout U.S. tolerates heat and humidity and produces a multitude of globe-shaped flowers summer through fall. Use 'Gnome Purple' for dwarf bedding variety (8").
Hyacinth *Hyacinthus orientalis* 'Woodstock'	Red-purple flowers Perennial (Z 4–8) H 8–12"; S–PS	Fall-planted bulb produces a spring-flowering thick and formal-looking spike densely covered in fragrant, bell-shaped flowers. Needs good drainage.
Japanese Iris *Iris ensata* 'Wine Ruffles'	Red violet flowers Perennial (Z 4–9) H 4'; S–PS	Japanese iris have large flowers with flattened tops and large sword-like leaves. They prefer rich, acidic soil and need moist, well-drained conditions. This cultivar has 9" flowers with velvety falls.
Love-Lies-Bleeding *Amaranthus caudatus*. Also try: Polish amaranth *A. cruentus*	Burgundy flowers Annual H 3–5; S	Old-fashioned annual with dramatic, rope-like flowers cascading from tall stems. Great in bouquets. Polish amaranth has upright plumes and burgundy foliage.
New Guinea Impatiens *Impatiens* x *hybrida* 'Supersonic Violet Ice', 'Infinity Blushing Lilac'	Violet flowers Annual H 10–24"; PS–Sh	Large-petaled, long-spurred blooms on shade annual that tolerates some sun. Needs plenty of moisture and good drainage. Handsome lance-shaped leaves in whorls. Blooms all summer.
Ornamental Kale *Brassica oleracea* 'Red Chidori'. Also try: 'Peacock Red', 'Coral Queen'	Glaucous and magenta foliage Annual H 6–10"; S–PS	Compact, winter-hardy plants for fall containers and borders have fringed foliage with magenta centers. Best color in cool weather. 'Red Peacock' and 'Coral Queen' have finely serrated leaves.
Perilla *Perilla* x *hybrida* 'Magilla'	Purplish-green leaves with violet centers Annual H 3'; S–PS	Sun-loving annual grown for its colorful foliage, resembles coleus, but is a variety of the common herb shiso. Upright, bushy growth and strong performance all summer.
Periwinkle, Vinca *Catharanthus roseus* 'Raspberry Red Cooler', 'Orchid Cooler', 'Pacifica Burgundy'	Violet to magenta flowers Annual H 10–14"; S	Glossy mounds of foliage and bright pinwheel blooms from summer to fall are attributes of this heat-loving border plant. Plants succumb to disease with cool soils, poor drainage, and overhead watering.
Petunia *Petunia* x *violacea* 'Laura Bush'. Also try: *P.* 'Rambling Burgundy Chrome', 'Whispers Blue Rose', 'Purple Wave'	Violet flowers Annual H 18–24"; S–PS	Rugged disease-resistant variety produces numerous 1–$1^{1}/_{4}$" bell-shaped flowers even in summer's heat. Prefers fertile, well-drained soil. Tolerates alkalinity.
Pineapple Lily *Eucomis comosa* 'Sparkling Burgundy'	White flowers with dark burgundy foliage Perennial (Z 6–9) H 20"; S–PS	Clumping deciduous plant produces rosette of strap-like leaves and in summer has a 20" bloom stalk that resembles a miniature pineapple. Good in containers and borders.

QUICK FACTS COLOR DESCRIPTION: **Z** = Zone, **H** = Height, **S** = Sun, **PS** = Partial Sun or Partial Shade, **Sh** = Shade

PURPLE SMOKE TREE

TULIP 'NEGRITA'

VAN HOUTTE'S SALVIA 'PAUL'

Purple Coneflower *Echinacea purpurea* 'Ruby Star'. Also try: 'Magnus'	Carmine red flowers with orange centers Perennial (Z 3–8) H 35"; S–PS	Prairie natives, coneflowers offer long summer bloom and drought tolerance. 'Ruby Star' is an improved cultivar with large blooms and horizontal petals. 'Magnus' has deeper color and same horizontal petals.
Red Valerian *Centranthus ruber*	Reddish pink flowers Perennial (Z 4–9) H 1–3'; S–PS	Fluffy clusters of tiny flowers appear in spring and summer on bushy clumps of upright stems with glaucous foliage. Tolerates dry soils but performs best with moisture.
Rose campion *Lychnis coronaria*	Magenta-pink flowers Perennial (Z 4–8) H 1½–2½'; S–PS	In spring, fluorescent flowers emerge from basal rosettes of pubescent leaves. Though short-lived, plants can reseed to form attractive colonies.
Shrub Bushclover *Lespedeza bicolor* 'Little Buddy'. Also try: *L. thunbergii* 'Gibraltar'	Rose-purple flowers Perennial (Z 4–7) H 3'; S	Easily grown, this compact bush clover has graceful, arching habit and flowers late summer to fall. Good specimen for perennial border. 'Gibraltar', with 6' arching branches, is good cascading from wall.
Speedwell *Veronica spicata* 'Red Fox'	Reddish-pink flowers Perennial (Z 4–8) H 12–15"; S–PS	Flower clusters on terminal spikes bloom for several weeks in summer. Prefers rich, moist soil with good drainage.
Summer Phlox *Phlox paniculata* 'Robert Poore'	Violet pink flowers Perennial (Z 4–8) H 5–6'; S	Bold round flower clusters top multiple, upright stems in midsummer for several weeks. One of the most mildew resistant phlox.
Trailing Petunia *Calibrachoa* x *hybrida* 'Million Bells Trailing Magenta', 'Colorburst Burgundy'	Magenta flowers Perennial (Z 7) usually grown as annual H 4–6"; S–PS	Prostrate, petunia-like plant but with smaller leaves and flowers and better weather tolerance. Smothered in blooms all summer in cool climates. Elsewhere blooms best in spring and fall. Good in containers and baskets.
Tulip *Tulipa* Lily Group 'Ballade'. Also try: *T.* Triumph Group 'Barcelona', *T. humilis* 'Persian Pearl'	Magenta flowers with white edges Perennial bulbs (Z 3–7) treated as annuals in warm climates H 16–20"; S–PS	Tulips bloom in spring from bulbs planted in fall. 'Ballade' a lily-flowered tulip has flaring petal tips while 'Barcelona' is fuchsia with a rounded bloom. 'Persian Pearl' is just 6".
Van Houtte's Salvia *Salvia van houttei* 'Paul'. Also try: *S. splendens* 'Salsa Plum'	Burgundy to plum flowers Annual H 4–5'; S–PS	Floriferous habit and rapid growth make this salvia premium for summer to fall beauty. Likes moist, well-drained soil. 'Salsa Plum' is useful bedding variety at 14".
Verbena *Verbena* x *hybrida* 'Tapien Blue-Violet'. Also try: 'Temari Violet'	Violet flowers Annual H 3–8"; S–PS	Hybrid verbena with mildew-resistant fern-leaf foliage and round flower clusters with a vigorous trailing habit. Good for baskets or as ground cover. 'Temari Violet' is 5–12" tall.
Zinnia *Zinnia elegans* 'Benary's Giant Purple'	Violet purple flowers Annual H 3–4'; S	Dahlia-shaped zinnia on tall, well-branched plant is excellent source for cut flowers as well as garden color. Provide good air circulation and avoid overhead watering.

MAGENTA | COOL COLORS

WARM
COLOR EXPRESSIONS

YELLOW, APRICOT, ORANGE, RED

Words fail to describe what a heart-pounding experience it is to drive through the forested hills of the Northeast during the peak of autumn color. You can almost feel the vibrating energy of trees adorned in their most vivid hues of scarlet, orange, and gold. It's no wonder we think of hot colors as energetic and assertive. Summer's restful, verdant greens are pushed aside as these blazing colors sweep across the landscape. The cracking reds and sizzling oranges seem to scream the loudest for attention, almost as if they sense that their time is short. In winter's landscape, warm colors are often hard to find, appearing as mere flickers in the garden's canvas as twigs, berries, and broadleaf evergreen foliage. Spring's cool hues are sparked with accents of yellow, peach, and red as early flowering bulbs, trees, and shrubs emerge. In summer, as temperatures and the colors in our gardens cook up, reds, oranges, and yellows take on a larger role in the landscape, but it is in autumn when these fiery colors pull out all the stops and put on their most spectacular show. The primal pull of being drawn to these colors is within us just as we are attracted to the light and warmth of a campfire. They add zest and urgency to any composition in a way that arrests and holds our attention.

Nature offers the best guide as you dip into these hot buckets of color to paint your garden. Use them sparingly at first, slowly building their role through the seasons until it is autumn, when too much is just enough. Because of their spirited qualities through most of the growing season, it is wise to find the tipping point in your color combinations when hot colors overwhelm the garden and your senses. For much of the year they are more effective as an accent to other color harmonies.

As explained in Section Two, textural interest is as important as color selection. This is especially pertinent when it comes to exploring the hot shades. Attention-grabbing flowers in fiery tones of red, orange, apricot, and yellow are best appreciated when balanced by a supporting cast of contrasting foliage. Shimmering greens, silvery grays, and blue foliage plants add a quiet luminescence when threaded among vivid flowers. Variegated leaves with soft tones of gold and hints of red, along with soft yellow striped rustling grasses such as *Miscanthus sinensis* 'Zebrinus' layer in other colors, movement, and sound.

Groupings of fiery colors can be blended into a larger border setting by interweaving their edges with muted shades of apricots, buffs, and creams, or bronzed autumn shades of russet, copper, and cinnamon. The repeated use of a distinctive foliage shrub between compositions of warm colors creates continuity and establishes a color thread through this rich tapestry. Warm colors are provocateurs, luring us in with a seductive embrace. It is a spectrum of colors that is more dynamic and engaging, less distant and aloof, than cooler colors.

Yellow Shrubs

Witch hazel: *Hamamelis* x *intermedia* 'Arnold's Promise'
Winter jasmine: *Jasminum nudiflorum*
Forsythia: *Forsythia intermedia* 'Lynwood', 'Goldtide'
Oregon grape holly: *Mahonia aquifolia*
Leatherleaf mahonia: *Mahonia bealei*
Scotch broom: *Cytisus scoparius* 'Moonlight'
Warminister broom: *Cytisus* x *praecox* 'Allgold'
Golden chain tree: *Laburnum* x *watereri* 'Vossii'
Cinquefoil: *Potentilla fruticosa* 'Katherine Dykes',
'Gold Drop', 'Jackman's Variety'
Winter hazel: *Corylopsis*
Oleander: *Nerium oleander* 'Double Yellow'
Woadwaxen: *Genista lydia*
Cassia: *Cassia bicapsularis*; *C. splendida* 'Golden'
Esperanza: *Tecoma stans* 'Gold Star'
Butterfly bush: *Buddleia* 'Honeycomb'
Silver wattle: *Acacia dealbata*
Japanese kerria: *Kerria japonica* 'Pleniflora'
St. John's wort: *Hypericum prolificum* 'Hidcote'

Yellow

Yellow is reflected in so many of the things around us: sunshine, lemons, butter, and the first blooms of spring. After a long gray winter, the cheerful yellows of forsythia and daffodils are served up like appetizers to the gardener hungry for color. Throughout the year, yellow takes on different qualities depending on the light in which it is viewed. In bright sunshine it shimmers brilliantly, while in filtered shade it glows with a soft luminescence. The range of shades found in the plants themselves vary widely, from the sharpness of clear lemon into the softness of creamy vanilla and through the warmth of rich gold.

Yellow hues are apparent year round, but are most noticeable in spring and fall, so they tend to bookend the growing season. The way I use them in the garden from March through November varies with the season. In the spring I can't get enough yellow with banks of blooming forsythia, happy-faced daffodils, and large-cupped tulips. As spring turns to summer, I use them in my borders and containers with a lighter hand. Too much yellow, especially in shrubs and other types of foliage, can give the appearance that the plants are in poor health. Of course, this effect varies depending on where you live. In foggy, rain-drenched sections of the country, bright yellow vegetation illuminates a border like sunshine falling in shafts of light on favored plants. However in bright, sunny locations, yellow appears brassy in large quantities.

Yellow is particularly effective when used to draw attention to a focal point. Both people and insects recognize this characteristic. Yellow frequently appears in flower blossoms as bee guides. Stamens of flowers are often touched in yellow or blossoms are streaked in yellow to create patterns that serve almost as lights on a landing strip guiding insects to the pollen. I use yellow in

Left: From late winter to early spring, the bright yellow blooms of a forsythia bush are welcome sparks of life. I like them best preserved in their graceful, fountainlike form, rather than sheared into balls or boxes. **Opposite, above left:** A partially shaded path is flooded with spring sunshine in the form of primrose tulips, columbine, pansies, and a chartreuse carpet of golden creeping Jenny. Blue nemesia weaves levelheadedly through this rowdy crowd, providing a cool contrast. **Opposite, above right:** Though small in size, cyclamineus daffodils are big in beauty. Their floriferous early-spring display, robust dependability, and charming reflexed petals make them one of my favorites. **Opposite, below left:** The round blooms of yellow 'Million Bells' calibrachoa cascade across the path, mingling in the border with salvia and artemisia. Its trailing form makes it a good choice for hanging baskets and containers. **Opposite, below right:** Few names are as fitting as the sunflower. Their seeds can be planted sequentially to create blooms from early to late summer.

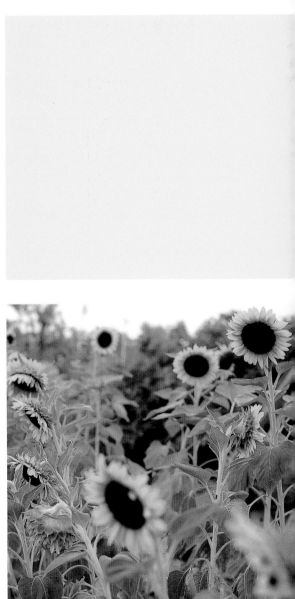

my summer garden in a similar fashion, as an accent to set off other plants or highlight certain spots in a border or container.

Two daylilies that add beautiful yellow accents to a flower border are 'Hyperion', with lemon-yellow flowers that bloom on tall (40-inch) scapes, and 'Happy Returns', a shorter variety (18 inches) with clear yellow flowers that rebloom through the summer. Combine 'Happy Returns' with blue salvia, pale butter-yellow lantana, silver artemisia, and blue plumbago for a lively display. The center of the butter-cream lantana plays off the yellow daylily.

Yellow Plant Combinations

SPRING *(sun)*
Forsythia
Mixed daffodils
Grape hyacinths

SUMMER *(sun)*
'New Gold' lantana
Persian shield (*Strobilanthes*)
'Imperial Blue' plumbago

FALL *(sun)*
'First Light' willow leaf sunflower
(*Helianthus angustifolius* 'First Light')
'Purple Dome' aster
'Heavy Metal' panicum

Yellow Roses

'Lady Banks'
'Mermaid'
'Jude Obscure'
'Rise and Shine'
'Elina'
'Golden Showers'
'Graham Thomas'
'Alberic Barbier'
'Reve d'Or'
'Celine Forestier'

Apricot

Apricot, peach, light salmon—whatever name you assign to this color, it can only be described as delicious. In the gardening world it is one of the most sought after colors because of all the sensory responses that it conjures up. Certainly it is the softer and less extroverted side of orange, but this alone does not truly explain its seductive qualities. It is a complex color that dazzles us with a wide range of shades and tints. Residing somewhere midway between the soft beauty of pink and the bold energy of orange, it seems to express both simultaneously. I confess I'm completely besotted by the color and compelled to try any plant with apricot in its name, and believe me, there are lots of them.

Above: From peach to apricot to salmon, many daylily cultivars are available to help you add color to your garden. Daylilies are a gardener's dream, offering glorious flowers and a long season of bloom (although individual flowers last but a day). Add to the list a robust disposition that makes them easy to transplant, low maintenance, an ability to multiply quickly, and resistance to pests. **Opposite:** Yellow 'Hyperion' daylilies commingle with pink cosmos to create a light mix of colors.

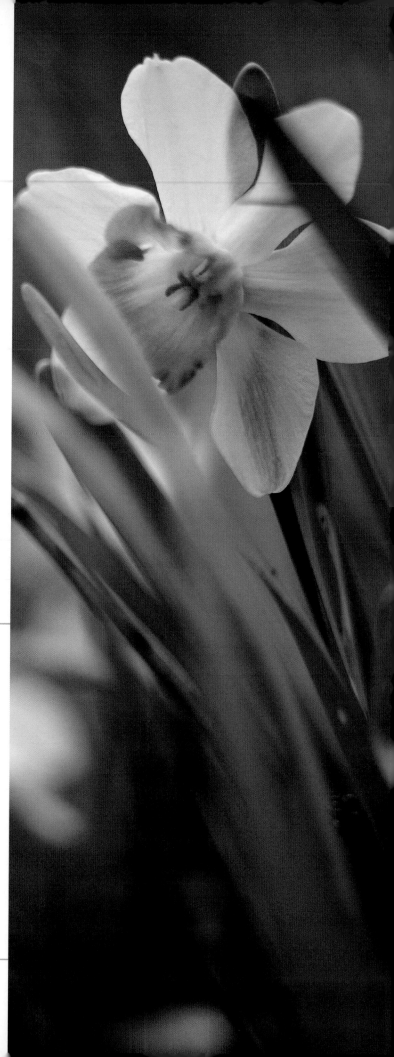

Like purple to lavender on the cool side, apricot seems to be more compatible with a wider range of colors than its warm cousins. For example, apricot is a natural with lavender and purple, especially the closer it moves to orange. It blends easily with blue, especially if you throw in some white and silvery foliage. Its relationship to cool reds and pinks may require some finesse, but proper compatibility of proportion and intensity in the blend can lead to lovely results.

When combining apricot with warm colors, it can bridge the gap from the richest orange to clear yellow. I think it is stunning with soft yellow and cream, but it is at its best when paired with the neutrals. Apricot is sophisticated with brown, sexy with black, elegant with silver, and downright sassy when brought into the extroverted company of chartreuse.

My undiminished passion for this color is even more insatiable when it is attached to roses. As many of the flowers evolve from bud to full bloom, they display the full color range of this hue, everything from near orange to soft pink.

Besides old-fashioned roses, another of my unabashed apricot-colored flower favorites is the daffodil. Its simple and carefree beauty symbolizes all the possibilities of spring. While they are often referred to as "pink" daffodils, they are actually closer to apricot in color. 'Salome' is a variety with a peach-colored trumpet that is surrounded by a creamy white collar, a combination so luscious you could eat it with a spoon!

Apricot Roses

'Perle d'Or'

'Evelyn'

'Abraham Darby'

'Colette'

'Crepescule'

'Albertine'

'Alister Stella Gray'

'Gruss an Aachen'

'Felicia'

'Cornelia'

'Marie van Houtte'

'Leotine Gervais'

'Mutabilis'

Apricot Daffodils

'Accent'

'Salome'

'Chromacolor'

'Mon Cherie'

'Eastern Dawn'

'Faith'

'Pink Charm'

'Precocious'

'Passionale'

'Bell Song'

Apricot Plant Combinations

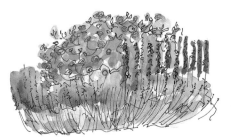

SPRING *(sun)*

'Apricot Beauty' foxglove

'Purple Sensation' allium

Lamiastrum

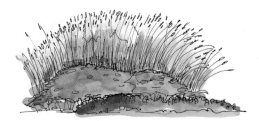

SUMMER *(sun)*

'Abraham Darby' rose

Russian sage

'Bressingham Spire' monkshood

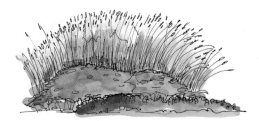

FALL *(sun)*

'Camille' chyrsanthemum

'Universal Lavender' pansies

Fountain grass

Opposite: The cup of the daffodil 'Bell Song' (*Narcissus jonquilla*) is a delicate salmon pink. **Above left:** 'Abraham Darby' is one of the many beautiful Austin English roses. **Below left:** A range of warm copper, rust, and apricot emanates from this coleus, making it compatible with the spiky bulbine frutecens in the foreground as well as the slender orange blossoms of the 'Firecracker' cuphea in the rear.